THE COMMUNITY RULE

EARLY JUDAISM AND ITS LITERATURE

Rodney A. Werline, General Editor

Editorial Board:
Randall D. Chesnutt
Kelley N. Coblentz Bautch
Maxine L. Grossman
Jan Joosten
James S. McLaren
Carol Newsom

Number 51

THE COMMUNITY RULE

A CRITICAL EDITION WITH TRANSLATION

Sarianna Metso

with a contribution by

Michael A. Knibb

and the assistance of

Chad Martin Stauber

SBL PRESS

Atlanta

Copyright © 2019 by Society of Biblical Literature

All rights reserved. No part of this work may be reproduced or transmitted in any form or by any means, electronic or mechanical, including photocopying and recording, or by means of any information storage or retrieval system, except as may be expressly permitted by the 1976 Copyright Act or in writing from the publisher. Requests for permission should be addressed in writing to the Rights and Permissions Office, SBL Press, 825 Houston Mill Road, Atlanta, GA 30329 USA.

Library of Congress Cataloging-in-Publication Data

Names: Metso, Sarianna, author, translator.
Title: The community rule : a critical edition with translation / by Sarianna Metso.
Other titles: Manual of discipline.
Description: Atlanta : SBL Press, [2019] | Series: Early Judaism and its literature ; 51 | Includes bibliographical references and index. | Text in Hebrew with English translation; introduction and critical matter in English.
Identifiers: LCCN 2019043723 (print) | LCCN 2019043724 (ebook) | ISBN 9780884140566 (paperback) | ISBN 9780884140580 (hardback) | ISBN 9780884140573 (ebook)
Subjects: Manual of discipline—Criticism, interpretation, etc. | Manual of discipline—Criticism, Textual.
Classification: LCC BM488.M3 M478 2019 (print) | LCC BM488.M3 (ebook) | DDC 296.1/55—dc23
LC record available at https://lccn.loc.gov/2019043723
LC ebook record available at https://lccn.loc.gov/2019043724

Contents

Acknowledgments vii

Sigla ix

Abbreviations x

Introduction

    Rationale 1

    Discovery and Publication of Serek Manuscripts 1

    Physical Descriptions and Character of the Manuscripts 2

    Theoretical and Methodological Considerations 6

    Volume Layout 7

    Bibliography 9

Hebrew Text and English Translation

    Column I 16

    Column II 18

    Column III 20

    Column IV 22

    Column V 26

    Column VI 32

    Column VII 38

    Column VIII 40

    Column IX 46

    Column X 50

    Column XI 56

Acknowledgments

The impetus for this work arose in the many discussions I have had with colleagues and students sparked by The Hebrew Bible: A Critical Edition project (HBCE) and by the movement toward creating critical editions of ancient Jewish texts. I am grateful for the conversations and encouragement to take the learnings from the HBCE project and apply them to nonscriptural Dead Sea Scrolls. In particular, I want to thank Judith Newman and Rodney Werline for inviting me to contribute to the Early Judaism and its Literature series and SBL Press Director Bob Buller and his team for bringing this work to publication. I hope that this volume is an early effort toward new editorial exploration of ancient Jewish scribalism.

Two academic groups of which I have had the privilege of being a member have been particularly generative for my work: the Scrollery Colloquium, a collaborative forum between the University of Toronto and McMaster University for faculty and graduate students whose research focuses on or integrates the Dead Sea Scrolls; and the Biblical Colloquium, a scholarly organization founded at Johns Hopkins University. I am grateful for the feedback and stimulus I have received at the yearly gatherings of these two groups from both young and seasoned scholars whose work I admire.

I am deeply indebted to Chad Stauber, who has assisted me in this project from the very beginning. His technical skills and scholarly input have greatly contributed to this volume. I also want to thank my graduate student assistants, John Screnock and James Tucker, for their many dedicated hours.

The scholarship of Professor Michael A. Knibb has inspired me ever since I was an exchange student at Kings College, University of London. He graciously agreed to allow me to use his translation in this volume with adaptations reflecting the Cave 4 evidence, and Cambridge University Press granted the publisher's permission.

I am profoundly grateful for the support and encouragement of Eugene Ulrich, my husband and colleague, and for his expert advice regarding especially the palaeography of the Serek manuscripts.

This project has been generously supported with an Insight Development Grant from the Social Sciences and Humanities Research Council of Canada. I also want to acknowledge the financial and scholarly support from the Department of Historical Studies and the Department of Near and Middle Eastern Civilizations at the University of Toronto.

Sigla

[ ]	lacuna in all extant manuscripts
[כול]	reconstructed text based on the same or similar phrase attested elsewhere in Serek manuscripts
⌜א⌝	non-copy-text reading, either a reading supplied by a parallel manuscript or a textual emendation
אל	variant in the text
א̇	letter damaged; reading substantially certain
א̊	letter seriously damaged; reading uncertain
○	letter damaged to the point of being unidentifiable
<א>	deletion by scribe
א̇	cancellation dots; scribal erasure of a letter
כֿיל	correction by scribe; insertion of superlinear letter
vacat	intentional space left in the text
]	separator after lemma in the apparatus
כֿ	overstroke indicating indistinguishable forms of certain letters (מ/ס, ו/י, ד/כ, פ/ף, ץ/צ)
⌐	*Paragraphos* sign, used by scribes usually to draw attention to the end of a section in the manuscript
𐤀 𐤁 𐤂	other marginal scribal signs

ABBREVIATIONS

ASOR	American Schools of Oriental Research
BASORSup	Bulletin of the American Schools of Oriental Research Supplements
BZAW	Beihefte zur Zeitschrift für die alttestamentliche Wissenschaft
BZNW	Beihefte zur Zeitschrift für die neutestamentliche Wissenschaft
CBET	Contributions to Biblical Exegesis and Theology
CCWJCW	Cambridge Commentaries on Writings of the Jewish and Christian World 200 BC to AD 200
CQS	Companion to the Qumran Scrolls
DCLS	Deuterocanonical and Cognate Literature Studies
DJD	Discoveries in the Judaean Desert
DSD	*Dead Sea Discoveries*
EJL	Early Judaism and Its Literature
HBCE	The Hebrew Bible: A Critical Edition
JJS	*Journal of Jewish Studies*
JSJSup	Supplements to the Journal for the Study of Judaism in the Persian, Hellenistic, and Roman Periods
JSP	*Journal for the Study of the Pseudepigrapha*
LNTS	The Library of New Testament Studies
LSTS	The Library of Second Temple Studies
RB	*Revue biblique*
RBS	Resources for Biblical Study
RevQ	*Revue de Qumrân*
STDJ	Studies on the Texts of the Desert of Judah
TCSt	Text-Critical Studies
TSAJ	Texts and Studies in Ancient Judaism
VTSup	Supplements to Vetus Testamentum
col(s).	column(s)
frag(s).	fragment(s)
pl(s).	plate(s)

For reasons of brevity, Arabic rather than Roman numerals have been used in the apparatus for both column and line numbers when referring to 1QS. Elsewhere, when referring only to a column without a line number, the more common convention of using Roman numerals has been employed.

Introduction

The discovery of the Dead Sea Scrolls has greatly increased the knowledge of how texts were produced and transmitted in Jewish antiquity. This, in turn, is transforming the way new editions of ancient Jewish texts are conceived. This volume presents a critical edition of the Hebrew manuscripts of the Community Rule (Serek Hayaḥad), a document that was foundational for the life and self-understanding of the group behind the Dead Sea Scrolls. The edition contains the critical text with an apparatus of textual variants and additional notes on the manuscripts as well as an English translation.

Rationale

With the increased knowledge provided by the scrolls, scholars preparing new editions of scriptural books have already published a significant body of work that has generated a theoretical and a methodological shift. Since no single transmitted manuscript has escaped scribal errors and changes, critical editions are replacing diplomatic editions. A major example is The Hebrew Bible: A Critical Edition series, a project now underway (see Hendel 2016). Instead of printing a diplomatic text (Codex St. Petersburg) with its inevitable scribal errors and accretions, the goal of that project is to present an archetype for each book, that is, the latest attainable version of the text behind the existing manuscript witnesses. Through the apparatus, the volumes aim at describing the growth of the book through time. This edition of the Serek Hayaḥad attempts to reflect this shift and mirror the current editorial practices underway in the field. Although the chronological span is shorter and the amount of manuscript material tends to be much smaller as regards nonscriptural material, there is no theoretical reason not to strive for a similar approach, while acknowledging that there are some practical limitations to the task.

The scribal practice exhibited in the scrolls demonstrates that, although the ancient scribes usually attempted to copy the earlier text accurately, occasionally some scribes developed the text they were copying in creative ways. This was the case in both scriptural and nonscriptural works; the evidence reveals that the scribes did not differentiate between the two. Both types, as transmitted, had not been authored by single persons whose work remained unchanged but had been community-generated. The texts grew and developed as they were handed down, and different versions could exist side by side for lengthy periods of time. A corollary is that the line separating redaction criticism from textual criticism is blurred.

This situation raises serious questions, theoretically and methodologically, about how to present critical editions. Most editions of the individual scrolls were published separately. That is, the fragments that constituted one manuscript were usually published in a volume with the editions of other works found in the same cave. For example, since manuscripts of Psalms and the Community Rule were found in Caves 1, 4, 5, and 11, the different editions of the manuscripts were spread over several volumes unrelated to each other. Scholarly study and conclusions often focus on the most extensively preserved manuscript (e.g., 1QS) without the benefit of the scattered smaller fragments, irrespective of whether the best-preserved manuscript was the most authentic copy or whether the leaders and members of the community considered it the most definitive. The challenge, then, is how to present the full evidence of the preserved text.

Discovery and Publication of Serek Manuscripts

When Cave 1 was discovered in 1947, the Community Rule was among the first seven scrolls found. The manuscript, subsequently labeled 1QS, contained eleven virtually complete columns. Millar Burrows in 1951 published its *editio princeps* with the title Manual of Discipline. The title that occurs in the first line of the manuscript, however, is Serek Hayaḥad, that is, the Community Rule, so that name is appropriately now widely used. Following the eleven columns of 1QS, there were two other shorter works, the Rule of the Congregation (1QSa) and the Blessings (1QSb). While they have usually been characterized as appendices to the text of 1QS, their exact relationship remains subject to debate, and scholarly opinions range from viewing the scroll of 1QS-1QSa-1QSb as a single work to considering 1QS, 1QSa, and 1QSb as three entirely different compositions. In considering that question, it should be noted that a number of scriptural manuscripts contain more than one book in a single scroll, for example, 4QGen-Exod[a], 4QpaleoGen-Exod[l], 4QExod-Lev[f], 1QpaleoLev-Num[a], 4QLev-Num[a], and 4QPent B, C, and D. The evidence seems to indicate that scribes copied nonscriptural material the same as scriptural material.

In 1952, Cave 4 revealed fragments of ten other manuscripts of the Community Rule. The first report of the Serek variants was issued as early as 1956 by J. T. Milik. Other preliminary discussions and editions followed (see the bibliography below), but the critical editions of 4QS[a–j] remained unpublished until 1998, when Philip Alexander and Geza Vermes published the ten manuscripts in volume 26 of the Discoveries in the Judaean Desert series.

Cave 5 offered one more small fragment surviving from yet a twelfth manuscript of the Community Rule (5Q11) (Milik 1962, 180–81). It contains parts of two columns with text paralleling parts of 1QS column II. Subsequently, from Cave 11, a fragment most likely belonging to a thirteenth manuscript (11Q29) was identified by Eibert Tigchelaar (2000, 285–92). He has also proposed that a tiny fragment from Cave 1, originally published as part of a manuscript entitled Tongues of Fire (1Q29) but now relabeled as 1Q29a, may provide a "a shorter and alternative version" of the Treatise on the Two Spirits, but the identification is not entirely certain.

Additional fragments surfaced of a manuscript entitled simply the Rule (5Q13) that quotes a phrase from the Community Rule. Sections of the Community Rule are also quoted in Cave 4 manuscripts of the Damascus Document (4Q266 frag. 10 and 4Q270 frag. 7), the Miscellaneous Rules (4Q265; formerly Serekh Dameseq), and possibly the Ritual of Marriage (4Q502 frag. 16). Other manuscripts related to the Community Rule are Rebukes Reported by the Overseer (4Q477; formerly Decrees), Communal Ceremony (4Q275), and Four Lots (4Q279).

Even a cursory reading of manuscript 1QS alone makes it clear that its text is an amalgamation of disparate passages most likely originating from a variety of sources. The fluid and heterogeneous character of the material is further emphasized by the parallel material from Caves 4, 5, and 11. The totality of the material associated with S raises, in fact, profound questions of how scribes and authors in Jewish antiquity conceived of a work (see Hendel 2016, 101–25; Hamidović 2016, 61–90, Jokiranta 2016, 611–35). It needs to be recognized that our usual, post-Enlightenment ideas of individual authorship and literary work are rather ill-fitting for the ancient world, and models that better reflect the realities of ancient text production are called for.

Physical Descriptions and Character of the Manuscripts

1QS

The Serek manuscript from Cave 1 Qumran (1QS) was among the very first scrolls found in 1947. Like the Great Isaiah Scroll (1QIsa[a]), which was part of the same discovery, it is virtually completely preserved, lacking only a few letters and words lost mostly from the lower edges of the scroll. Its text is inscribed on five leather sheets that were stitched together. It consists of eleven columns of approximately twenty-six lines each; the length of 1QS is circa 187 cm (ca. 6 feet, 2 inches), and the column height is approximately 25 cm (ca. 10 inches).

The scribe who copied 1QS is well known because he also copied 4QSam[c] and 4QTestimonia (Ulrich 2002, 187). As in those scrolls, he made a number of textual errors, corrections, and glosses; there are also marks in the margins, especially in columns VII and VIII. He often wrote medial forms of letters in final position and did not leave word spaces between words, especially between small words in a phrase.

The scroll had a handle sheet, and on its verso there is one line with eight letters, [סר]ך היחד ומן[ ], giving the title of the scroll. The date of the scroll is 100–75 BCE determined palaeographically, and that date is confirmed both by radio-carbon tests (Bonani et al. 1991, 27–32) and by this scribe's marginal insertion at Isa 40:7b–8a in 1QIsa[a], which is dated 125–100 BCE (Ulrich 2015, 110 and 124).

New sections in the text are signified by blank spaces or marginal marks. Regarding blank spaces, a full line, or large part of a line, was intentionally left blank to mark a major break, especially for an introductory formula. A shorter interval occurs to mark smaller breaks. There are, however, occasional blank spaces that do not denote a new section. This was probably due to problems in the parent manuscript (the *Vorlage*) from which the scribe was copying. If it was marred or not well preserved, or if the scribe could not read the original clearly, it is understandable that he would leave the problematic places blank. For example, such blank spaces occur in columns VII and VIII, probably due to the poor condition of the *Vorlage*. Some spaces were later filled in, possibly by a second scribe, but by erasing some of the words originally written, he also created further intervals in the text. In contrast, the spaces at 6:10; 9:9, 14, 16, and the very large space of nearly three lines after 7:7 are due to defects in the leather used for 1QS, not to problems in the *Vorlage*.

Regarding marginal marks, two types are occasionally found in the right margin. A *paragraphos*, a horizontal line with a hook at the right side (similar to cryptic *ayin*), is placed in the margin, marking either the end of a section or an important sentence or paragraph; it usually occurs together with some blank space. The second type includes large signs, in the form of Paleo-Hebrew letters, in the margins of columns V, VII, and IX to mark sections of particular importance (for fuller discussion, see Tov 2004, 178–218).

The same scribe copied two other compositions, the Rule of the Congregation (1QSa) and Words of Blessing (1QSb), that were stitched to 1QS. Portions of seven columns are preserved, but the end of 1QSb is not preserved. The scroll had been rolled with its incipit in the center, and the part of the leather on which 1QSb was copied was thus on the more exposed outer layers. Therefore, we cannot know whether the combined scroll held more than its surviving eighteen columns. Since 1QSa and 1QSb were copied by the same scribe as 1QS, they are also dated 100–75 BCE.

1Q29a

Another manuscript from Cave 1, originally published as Tongues of Fire (1Q29), should be mentioned. Eibert Tigchelaar (2004, 529–47) subjected five of its tiny fragments to further analysis and tenuously proposed that the fragments may have derived from a copy of the Treatise on the Two Spirits (1Q29a). The small amount of text prevents establishing its identity, whether part of a lone-standing manuscript of the Treatise itself, a larger manuscript of S, or in a text that is only quoting the Treatise. In fact, he put a question mark in the title. But he recognized enough to suggest that, compared to 1QS, the fragments "indicate a shorter and alternative version." Some might question the chronology, since the script is Herodian and thus paleographically later than that of 1QS. But other examples, such as Jeremiah—where the later version (4QJer[a]), though copied circa 200 BCE, coexisted with the earlier version (4QJer[b]), copied circa 100–50 BCE—show that older and younger versions of a work can coexist for more than a century; note that this later date for an earlier version is the case also with 4QS[b] and 4QS[d].

4QpapS[a] (4Q255)

4QpapS[a] is a papyrus manuscript with text on both sides. The Serek text is on the side with fibers running horizontally, and 4QpapHodayot-Like Text B (4Q433a) is on the side with fibers running vertically (Schuller 1999, 237). 4QpapS[a] preserves only four fragments, though only two of the fragments contain clear parallels to 1QS. Fragment 1 has six partial lines of text at its top and left margins; they match the text at the upper left corner of the first 1QS column, 1QS 1:1–5. Fortunately, they supply a few words lost at the beginning of 1QS. Fragment 2 is the largest, with nine nearly complete lines at its top and right margins. It contains text parallel to 1QS 3:7–12, with only a few minute differences.

An additional fragment, listed as A in DJD 26, is a segment with five lines from a lower left corner of a column. Its text does not contain any direct parallel to 1QS, though the vocabulary is similar to that used in the Treatise on the Two Spirits (1QS 3:13–4:26), and it may loosely parallel the text in 1QS 3:20–25. Yet another fragment, B, has preserved only a few letters from each of five lines at the right margin, none of which help to identify the fragment. According to Frank Moore Cross, this manuscript, written in a crude cursive script, dates from the second half of the second century BCE, probably from the end of that century (Cross 1994, 57).

4QS^b (4Q256)

This leather manuscript has fifteen fragments preserved, some large, some tiny, combined and listed as fragments 1–8 in DJD 26. The fragments contain parallels for each of the main sections of 1QS except for the Treatise on the Two Spirits (1QS 3:13–4:26). The version of the Serek contained in 4QS^b, however, is shorter than that in 1QS. For example, the text in fragment 4 is shorter than its parallel in 1QS 5:1–20, and the text in fragments 5a–b is shorter than its parallel in 1QS 6:10–13. The surviving fragments allow only a partial reconstruction of the manuscript's layout, though the measurements of several columns can be calculated. In conjunction with the details available in the closely allied 4QS^d, the number of columns required for the version of the Serek contained in 4QS^b was probably twenty (Milik 1977, 76–77; Metso 1997, 24–26) to twenty-three (Alexander and Vermes 1998, 39).

An important feature to note is that, parallel to the end of the 1QS manuscript (11:22), the text of 4QS^b continues in fragment 8 with further text, which may be assumed to be a closing formula or the start of yet another text. Yet another possibility has been raised by Alexander and Vermes in DJD (1998, 26) regarding fragment 8. Noticing anomalies in the line spacing and the shape of *lamed*, they suggest that fragment 8 may not belong to the same manuscript at all. J. T. Milik (1977, 76–78) thought that the scribal hand of 4QS^b (*olim* 4QS^d) should be ascribed to the transitional period between the Hasmonean and Herodian scripts, dated to 50–25 BCE. Cross (1994, 57), partly overlapping with Milik, judged it as the typical early Herodian formal script of circa 30–1 BCE.

4QpapS^c (4Q257)

4QpapS^c is the second papyrus manuscript of the Serek. It is inscribed on both sides, with text of the Community Rule on the recto. The eight pieces preserved of 4QpapS^c provide parallels to parts of 1QS I–IV. Possibly, a ninth fragment belonging to this manuscript has been identified, for Eibert Tigchelaar (2004, 539) has proposed that a fragment previously assigned as 4Q502 fragment 16 actually belongs to 4QpapS^c. Except for two minute pieces difficult to identify and some features of orthography, the text of 4QpapS^c in the preserved parts is virtually identical to that in 1QS. A couple of words are written on the verso, but that text cannot be identified. Cross (1994, 57) dated the manuscript to circa 100–75 BCE, that is, roughly to the same period when 1QS was copied.

4QS^d (4Q258)

Of the Cave 4 copies of the Rule, 4QS^d preserves the largest individual fragments, though its component features are small. In the original manuscript the height of a column was only circa 8.0 cm containing only thirteen to fourteen lines, and the width was circa 10.7 cm. The beginning of column I of fragment 1 was quite probably also the beginning of the whole manuscript, judging from the fragment's right margin. That margin, at 2.1 cm wide, is twice the width of most margins, which usually measure 0.9–1.2 cm; moreover, that right margin displays no evidence of stitching. Remarkably, the opening text of 4QS^d starting at that right margin contains the rules for community life, corresponding to column V in 1QS. That is, 4QS^d does not have the first four columns of 1QS, comprising the introduction (1QS 1:1–18a), the liturgical passage (1:18b–3:12), and the Treatise on the Two Spirits (3:13–4:26). Those heterogeneous genres in 1QS columns I–IV, however, help explain their absence in 4QS^d, since the contents of 1QS columns V–XI are of a quite different nature. 4QS^d offers yet another valuable piece of information: its text matches that of 4QS^b, both exhibiting a shorter edition of the material in 1QS V–XI. Material reconstruction of these manuscripts helps demonstrate this shorter, and presumably earlier, edition of the text. A further noticeable feature in 4QS^d is that the name of God (אל) is written in the Paleo-Hebrew script at 8:9 and 9:8. Cross (1994, 57) judges the scribal hand as Herodian and dates it in the last third of the last century BCE.

4QS^e (4Q259)

A generous amount of fragments survives for 4QS^e. They all come from four columns with text paralleling 1QS VII–IX, so it cannot be determined whether the counterparts to 1QS I–IV had been part of this manuscript. Other important variations from 1QS, however, do appear. First, the text of column III is shorter than the corresponding text of 1QS: it does not have the twenty-four lines of text corresponding to 1QS 8:15b–9:11. Second, whereas 1QS concludes with a psalm in columns X–XI, column IV of 4QS^e has instead a calendrical text, 4QOtot. Milik (1976, 61–64) dated the manuscript—though he called it 4QS^b and called the calendrical text the Book of Signs or ha-'Ôtot—to the second half of the second century BCE. Cross (1994, 57), however, placed the late Hasmonean semicursive scribal hand a century later, circa 50–25 BCE.

4QS^f (4Q260)

The manuscript 4QS^f preserves seven fragments, though only six are visible in the PAM photographs included in DJD 26. The tiny seventh fragment is pictured on B-299964 and B-299965. They all show top margins and can be placed as the text of five columns corresponding to 1QS IX–X. The fragments exhibit the usual range of minor variants—orthographic, grammatical, and textual—but there is not enough to provide valuable information for the textual history of S. The script is from the early Herodian period, 30–1 BCE.

4QS^g (4Q261)

Small scraps remain of this manuscript: nineteen individual fragments, combined in DJD 26 (Alexander and Vermes 1998) as 1a–6e plus A, B, and C. Many of them do not exceed 1 cm in height or width, so it is difficult to read and identify them. The few identifiable parts correlate with 1QS V–VII, with some shorter and some longer variants. According to Cross (1994, 57), the script of the manuscript is semicursive and dates to circa 50–1 BCE.

4QS^h (4Q262)

Three fragments (1, A, and B) are listed in DJD 26 under the siglum 4QS^h, but only two (1 and A) can be confidently identified as belonging to the same manuscript. Fragment 1 has only three lines with complete words; they correspond to 1QS 3:4–6. The other two fragments (A and B) lack any correspondence with 1QS. Fragments 1 and A may not represent a copy of the Serek at all but a work that quotes a passage from it (Metso 2017, 158–59). The words in fragment 1, coincidently, are the same as those quoted in 5Q13. Cross (1994, 57), lists the script as a vulgar semiformal and assigns it to about the first half of the first century CE.

4QS^i (4Q263)

Only a single small fragment of 4QS^i survives, measuring 4.1 by 3.6 cm, with text corresponding to 1QS 6:1–4. Cross (1994, 57) attributed the script to the early Herodian period, 30–1 BCE.

4QS^j (4Q264)

In contrast to 4QS^i, although only a single fragment remains of this manuscript, its contents offer important evidence. It measures 4.4 by 4.3 cm, but since its script is small it preserves parts of ten lines that parallel the final lines of the Cave 1 Serek copy (1QS 11:14–22), suggesting that this may be the end of the manuscript. In addition, the leather fragment shows stitching along its left edge, strongly suggesting materially as well as its textually that it forms the conclusion of this copy. It cannot be determined whether the sheet following the stitching was a blank handle sheet or contained another composition. The Cave 1 copy continued with the Rule of the Congregation on the next sheet, and 4QS^b continued with some unidentifiable text. Cross (1994, 57) dates 4QS^j to the second half of the first century BCE.

5QS (5Q11)

Cave 5 also preserved a small trace of the Serek: a single fragment in Herodian script measuring 3.1 by 4.8 cm. It contains parts of six lines from two contiguous columns with stitching between them. The right column correlates with 1QS 2:4–7, but only about six letters on the left column are recognizable. It is possible that they parallel 1QS 2:12–14 (Milik 1962, 181). If so, and if its text matched that of 1QS, it would have held fourteen lines per column, but it would have contained small additions and omissions.

11QFragment Related to Serek Hayaḥad (11Q29)

Cave 11 furnished a number of documents, fortunately including one tiny fragment that contains only bits of two lines. That tiny text, however, parallels 1QS 7:18–19, though it has one variant. Due to the wording, it is impossible to determine whether it comes from the penal code of the Serek or rather from that in the Damascus Document or 4QMiscellaneous Rules (4Q265) (García Martínez, Tigchelaar, and van der Woude 1998, 433–434; Tigchelaar 2000, 285–92).

Theoretical and Methodological Considerations

For the purposes of creating a critical edition the material evidence of S poses profound theoretical and methodological challenges. Whereas 1QS is customarily used as the standard form of the work, it must be emphasized that other preserved forms present a surprisingly varied picture: the text of 4QS^b seems to have extended beyond the parallel of the last line of 1QS; and it appears that 4QS^d never contained a parallel of 1QS I–IV but commenced with a parallel to 1QS V. Only one fragment of 4QS^h presents a parallel to the text of 1QS, raising the question whether 4QS^h simply quotes the text of 1QS but in fact represents a different work altogether and should be compared to 5Q13 (Rule) that appears to quote the same passage of 1QS 3:4–5. A similar question can be raised of 1Q29a.

Differences abound at an even broader level. In 4QS^e, a calendrical text called 4QOtot is found instead of the final psalm of 1QS X–XI. Scholars have usually treated it as a separate work, but in the manuscript of 4QS^e it follows seamlessly a phrase overlapping with 1QS with no apparent break in the text. From the material perspective, then, it appears that the scribe copying 4QS^e did not treat the two as separate works. A question regarding the scribe's intent can also be raised in regard to the scroll of 1QS, 1QSa, and 1QSb: while 1QSa and 1QSb have usually been characterized as appendices to the text of 1QS, their exact relationship with 1QS remains an open question. In contrast to the case of 4QOtot, however, the scribe started 1QSa on a separate column and did the same with 1QSb.

Extensive overlaps with the text of 1QS are found in Cave 4 manuscripts of the Damascus Document (4Q266 frag. 10 and 4Q270 frag. 7) and the Miscellaneous Rules (4Q265; formerly Serek Dameseq). This raises the question of whether they should be treated as witnesses of the same text and therefore be included as variant editions of S.

It is thus evident that no clear boundaries existed in the minds of the scribes behind S as to what constituted the work. This level of fluidity in the material probably reflects the interplay of both oral and written traditions in the culture in which the scribes operated. Theoretically, then, we should refrain from attempting to formulate a notion of the Community Rule as a definite work. Practically, however, such an approach for an edition is not tenable, for decisions have to be made in regard to what material is included for presentation in the edition and what is not. This edition includes only manuscripts that have been labeled as S manuscripts in DJD editions, but the textual notes make occasional references to parallels in related texts.

Recent critical methods of editorial work on biblical books can suggest a more defensible process for other compositions. For example, the volumes of The Hebrew Bible: A Critical Edition—instead of presenting a diplomatic edition with its inevitable errors—survey all the relevant manuscripts and present as the critical text the archetype of the work (Hendel 2016, 22), selecting for each word the reading that was most likely "the earliest inferable state of the text" or that best explains the other variants. Secondary textual variants are listed in the critical apparatus along with a suggestion of how each variant arose. Some biblical books or sections of books exhibit variant editions, and these are presented side by side.

Focusing specifically on the Serek, what is the best way to present its evidence? The smaller manuscripts display major agreement with, but also variations from, 1QS in both content and form. As mentioned above, it appears that earlier and later editions of the work coexisted side by side for extensive periods. For example, 4QS^b and 4QS^d present an earlier version of the work, though their palaeographic date is later than the noticeably earlier date of 1QS, a later edition. Since parts of the Serek scrolls show variant editions, those sections should be presented side by side.

Volume Layout

In the preparation of the Hebrew text presented in this volume, all manuscripts of S have been consulted, although not each manuscript is individually fully presented. Rather, the edition presents the critical text, and any individual variants in other manuscripts to that critical text are recorded in the apparatus. For practical reasons, in the critical edition 1QS serves as the copy-text (for the definition of copy-text, see Hendel 2016, 29), while 4QS^d and 4QS^b alternate as the copy-text for the variant edition of 1QS columns V–VI and parts of columns VIII–X; this variant edition is printed in a separate, parallel column. For reasons of clarity, the line numbering and lemmata in the notes usually follow 1QS. This should not be taken as an indication of text-historical primacy of 1QS. Due to the fragmentary textual evidence, it is sometimes difficult to determine whether variants rise to the level of a different edition. This is the case in 4QS^g in particular; its affiliation is not certain.

A difficult practical question is raised by the material evidence of 4QS^e, for the twenty-four lines of text corresponding to 1QS 8:15b–9:11 were absent in that manuscript, and whereas 1QS concludes with a psalm in columns X–XI, 4QS^e instead had a calendrical text, 4QOtot. Clearly, the material of 4QS^e qualifies as a variant edition. The section labeled 4QOtot, however, is usually treated as a work of its own (4Q319), and for practical reasons this volume follows that convention, although theoretically and methodologically a more accurate depiction would be to present it as yet another parallel column.

In many respects, the volume reflects the current editorial practices underway in the field, especially in The Hebrew Bible: A Critical Edition project. The core of the work is the critical edition, printed on the left-hand page, normally in a single-column format but in a double-column format where a parallel version exists. Beneath the Hebrew text, textual variants are recorded in the apparatus along with textual notes and occasional brief discussions on the character of the variants. On each right-hand page, a corresponding English translation of the Hebrew text is provided.

Reconstructions in square brackets have been inserted in the critical text only in cases where none of the manuscripts in the S tradition has preserved the text. Generally, the approach to reconstructing in this volume has been minimalist rather than maximalist. Reconstructions for the lacunae have been provided only in cases when the same or a very similar phrase has been attested elsewhere in the S manuscripts or in cases where the phrase can be confidently reconstructed on the basis of its other frequent occurrences in the nonscriptural or scriptural manuscripts. The differing editions in columns V–VI and VIII–X pose a considerable challenge in this respect. In certain instances, the editions are close enough to reconstruct the lacunae with a high degree of confidence, but in many parts of the text the editions differ so significantly that reconstruction of large lacunae turns out to be quite a speculative undertaking. In these instances, no reconstructions have been provided.

The use of ceiling brackets signifies a non-copy-text reading, either a reading supplied by a parallel manuscript or, in rare cases, a textual emendation. Here, too, the approach has been rather conservative, and emendations have been suggested only in cases of a clear scribal error or grammatical mistake. These have been identified and explained in the apparatus.

Variant words and phrases are signaled by underlines. In the apparatus, the manuscripts in which they occur have been identified and their evidence presented, often with brief explanatory comments. Since it is widely recognized that scribes of the Second Temple period freely employed a variety of spelling practices and that orthographic variants rarely serve as reliable indicators of underlying textual traditions, purely orthographic variants are not listed. They are recorded only in cases where it is not entirely clear whether the orthography reflects a variant phonology or morphology.

The fragmentary character and extensive damage of many S manuscripts pose challenges for reading and analysis of many words, and irregularities in the shapes of letters, particularly in cases of scribal correction and erasure, present additional difficulties for transcribing the preserved text unambiguously in some cases. In certain manuscripts, medial and final forms of some letters are often not clearly distinguishable; quite often one encounters in final position medial-shaped letters written larger than usual. As is customary in many editions, the level of certainty has been indicated by using dots, circlets, and overstrokes placed above letters. Erasures and superlinears in the copy-texts have been maintained in the critical text for the purpose of illustrating the scribal process.

When preparing this edition, extensive use was made of the photographs available online in the Leon Levy Dead Sea Scroll Digital Library (https://www.deadseascrolls.org.il/home). This online library, created as a result of collaboration between the Israel Antiquities Authority and Google, provides access to high-quality photographs of the scrolls. Thanks to this invaluable resource, a number of debated readings have been confirmed or corrected in this edition, and a few entirely new readings have been proposed. The digital tools and resources now available have opened a new window into studying the work of the scribes of the Second Temple period, and it is reflected in the textual notes of this volume.

The translation in columns I–IX is by Michael A. Knibb in his volume *The Qumran Community* (1987), used with his kind permission and the permission of the publisher, Cambridge University Press. It has been slightly adapted to reflect the entire manuscript evidence behind the critical text. The translation in columns X–XI is original in this volume.

Bibliography

In addition to editions and translations, this bibliography focuses on questions pertaining to textual criticism and the literary history of the Community Rule.

Editions and Translations

Alexander, Philip S., and Geza Vermes. 1998. *Qumran Cave 4, XIX: Serekh Ha-Yaḥad and Two Related Texts.* DJD 26. Oxford: Clarendon.

Barthélemy, D., and J. T. Milik. 1955. *Qumran Cave I.* DJD 1. Oxford: Clarendon.

Brownlee, W. H. 1951. *The Dead Sea Manual of Discipline.* BASORSup 10–12. New Haven: American Schools of Oriental Research.

Burrows, Millar, John C. Trever, and William H. Brownlee, eds. 1951. *Plates and Transcription of the Manual of Discipline.* Fascicle 2 of vol. 2 of *The Dead Sea Scrolls of St. Mark's Monastery.* New Haven: American Schools of Oriental Research.

Charlesworth, James H. 1994. "Possible Fragment of the Rule of the Community (5Q11)." Pages 105–7 in *Rule of the Community and Related Documents.* Vol. 1 of *The Dead Sea Scrolls: Hebrew, Aramaic, and Greek Texts with English Translations.* Edited by James H. Charlesworth. Tübingen: Mohr Siebeck; Louisville: John Knox.

———. 1996. *The Dead Sea Scrolls: Rule of the Community, Photographic Multi-language Edition.* Philadelphia: American Interfaith Institute/World Alliance.

Cross, Frank Moore, David Noel Freedman, and James A. Sanders, eds. 1972. *Scrolls from Qumran Cave 1: The Great Isaiah Scroll, the Order of the Community, the Pesher to Habakkuk from Photographs by John C. Trever.* Jerusalem: Albright Institute of Archaeological Research and the Shrine of the Book.

Dimant, Devorah. 2014. "1Q28 (1QS)." Pages 40–53 in *Dead Sea Scrolls Handbook.* Edited by Devorah Dimant, Donald W. Parry, and Geraldine I. Clements. Leiden: Brill.

García Martínez, Florentino, and Eibert J. C. Tigchelaar. 1997–1998. "1QS," "4Q255-264," "5Q11," and "11Q29?" Pages 68–98 and 510–44 in vol. 1 and 1132–35 and 1308–9 in vol. 2 of *The Dead Sea Scrolls Study Edition.* 2 vols. Leiden: Brill.

García Martínez, Florentino, Eibert J. C. Tigchelaar, and Adam S. van der Woude. 1998. "11QFragment Related to Serekh ha-Yaḥad." Pages 433–34 + pl. L in *Qumran Cave 11.II: 11Q2–18, 11Q20–31.* DJD 23. Oxford: Clarendon.

Guilbert, Pierre. 1961. "La Règle de la Communauté." Pages 9–80 in vol. 1 of *Les Textes de Qumran traduits et annotés.* Edited by J. Carmignac and P. Guilbert. 2 vols. Paris: Letouzey et Ané.

Habermann, Abraham M. 1959. *Megilloth Midbar Yehudah: The Scrolls of the Judaean Desert, Edited with Vocalization, Introduction, Notes and Concordance.* Jerusalem: Machbaroth LeSifruth.

Licht, Jacob. 1961. *The Rule Scroll: A Scroll from the Wilderness of Judaea, 1QS, 1QSa, 1QSb; Text, Introduction and Commentary*. Jerusalem: Bialik Institute.

Lohse, Eduard. 1986. *Die Texte aus Qumran: Hebräisch und Deutsch, mit Masoretischer Punktation, Übersetzung, Einführung und Anmerkungen*. 4th ed. Munich: Kösel-Verlag.

Martone, Corrado. 1995. *La "Regola Della Comunità": Edizione Critica*. Quaderni di Henoch 8. Torino: Silvio Zamorani.

Medico, Henri E. del. 1951. *Deux manuscrits Hébreux de la Mer Morte: Essai de traduction du "Manuel de Discipline" et du "Commentaire d'Habakkuk" avec notes et commentaires*. Paris: Geuthner.

Metso, Sarianna. 1997. *The Textual Development of the Qumran Community Rule*. STDJ 21. Leiden: Brill.

Milik, J. T. 1962. "5Q11 Règle de la Communauté." Pages 180–81 + pl. XXXVIII in *Les "Petites Grottes" de Qumran*. Edited by M. Baillet, J. T. Milik, and R. de Vaux. DJD 3. Oxford: Clarendon.

Parry, Donald W., and Emanuel Tov, eds. 2004. *Texts Concerned with Religious Law, Exegetical Texts and Parabiblical Texts*. Vol. 1 of *The Dead Sea Scrolls Reader*. 2nd ed. Leiden: Brill.

Qimron, Elisha. 2010. *The Hebrew Writings*. Vol. 1 of *The Dead Sea Scrolls*. Jerusalem: Yad Ben-Zvi.

———. 2018. *A Grammar of the Hebrew of the Dead Sea Scrolls*. Jerusalem: Yad Yizhak Ben-Zvi.

Qimron, Elisha, and James H. Charlesworth. 1994a. "Cave IV Fragments (4Q255–264 = 4QS MSS A-J)." Pages 53–103 in *Rule of the Community and Related Documents*. Vol. 1 of *The Dead Sea Scrolls: Hebrew, Aramaic, and Greek Texts with English Translations*. Edited by James H. Charlesworth. Tübingen: Mohr Siebeck; Louisville: John Knox.

———. 1994b. "Rule of the Community (1QS)." Pages 1–51 in *Rule of the Community and Related Documents*. Vol. 1 of *The Dead Sea Scrolls: Hebrew, Aramaic, and Greek Texts with English Translations*. Edited by James H. Charlesworth. Tübingen: Mohr Siebeck; Louisville: John Knox.

Schuller, Eileen. 1999. "433a 4QHodayot-Like Text B." Pages 237–45 in *Qumran Cave 4.XX: Poetical and Liturgical Texts, Part 2*. Edited by Esther Chazon et al. DJD 29. Oxford: Clarendon.

Vermes, Geza. 2004. *The Complete Dead Sea Scrolls in English*. Rev. ed. London: Penguin.

Wernberg-Møller, Preben C. H. 1957. *The Manual of Discipline: Translated and Annotated with an Introduction*. STDJ 1. Leiden: Brill.

Wise, Michael O., Martin G. Abegg Jr., and Edward M. Cook. 1996. *The Dead Sea Scrolls: A New Translation*. London: HarperCollins.

Secondary Studies

Alexander, Philip S. 1996. "The Redaction-History of the Serekh Ha-Yaḥad: A Proposal." *RevQ* 17:437–56.

Arata Mantovani, Piera. 1983. "La stratificazione letteraria della Regola della Comunità: A proposito di uno studio recente." *Henoch* 5:69–91.

Baumgarten, Joseph M. 1992. "The Cave 4 Versions of the Qumran Penal Code." *JJS* 42:268–76.

Bockmuehl, Markus. 1998. "Redaction and Ideology in the Rule of the Community (1QS/4QS)." *RevQ* 19:541–60.

Bonani, G. et al. 1991. "Radiocardbon Dating of the Dead Sea Scrolls." *Atiqot* 20:27–32.

Charlesworth, James H., and Brent A. Strawn. 1996. "Reflections on the Text of Serekh Ha-Yaḥad Found in Cave IV." *RevQ* 17:403–35.

Clines, David J. A. *The Dictionary of Classical Hebrew*. 9 vols. Sheffield: Sheffield Phoenix Press, 1993–2014.

Collins, John J. 2010. *Beyond the Qumran Community: The Sectarian Movement of the Dead Sea Scrolls*. Grand Rapids: Eerdmans.

Cross, Frank Moore. 1961. "The Development of the Jewish Scripts." Pages 133–202 in *The Bible and the Ancient Near East*. Edited by G. E. Wright. Garden City, NY: Doubleday.

———. 1994. "Paleographical Dates of the Manuscripts." Page 57 in *Rule of the Community and Related Documents*. Vol. 1 of *The Dead Sea Scrolls: Hebrew, Aramaic, and Greek Texts with English Translations*. Edited by James H. Charlesworth. Tübingen: Mohr Siebeck; Louisville: John Knox.

Davies, Philip R. 1992. "Redaction and Sectarianism in the Qumran Scrolls." Pages 152–63 in *The Scriptures and the Scrolls: Studies in Honour of A. S. van der Woude on the Occasion of His 65th Birthday*. Edited by F. García Martínez, A. Hilhorst, and C. J. Labuschagne. VTSup 49. Leiden: Brill.

Debel, Hans. 2011. "Rewritten Bible, Variant Literary Editions and Original Text(s): Exploring the Implications of a Pluriform Outlook on the Scriptural Tradition." Pages 65–92 in *Changes in Scripture: Rewriting and Interpreting Authoritative Traditions in the Second Temple Period*. Edited by Hanne von Weissenberg, Juha Pakkala, and Marko Marttila. BZAW 419. Berlin: de Gruyter.

Dimant, Devorah. 2006. "The Composite Character of the Qumran Sectarian Literature as an Indication of Its Date and Provenance." *RevQ* 22:615–30.

Fitzmyer, Joseph A. 1990. *The Dead Sea Scrolls: Major Publications and Tools for Study*. RBS 20. Atlanta: Scholars Press.

———. 2008 *A Guide to the Dead Sea Scrolls and Related Literature*. Rev. and exp. ed. Studies in the Dead Sea Scrolls and Related Literature. Grand Rapids: Eerdmans.

Gagnon, Robert A. 1992. "How Did the Rule of the Community Obtain Its Final Shape? A Review of Scholarly Research." *JSP* 10:61–79.

Garnet, Paul. 1997. "Cave 4 MS Parallels to 1QS 5.1–7: Towards a Serek Text History." *JSP* 15:67–78.

Gillihan, Yonder Moynihan. 2012. *Civic Ideology, Organization, and Law in the Rule Scrolls: A Comparative Study of the Covenanters' Sect and Contemporary Voluntary Associations in Political Context*. STDJ 97. Leiden: Brill.

Guilbert, Pierre. 1958. "Deux écritures dans les colonnes VII et VIII de la *Règle de la Communauté*." *RevQ* 1:199–212.

———. 1961. "La Règle de la Communauté." Pages 9–80 in vol. 1 of *Les textes de Qumran traduits et annotés*. Edited by J. Carmignac and P. Guilbert. 2 vols. Paris: Letouzey et Ané.

Hamidović, David, 2016. "Living *Serakhim*: Process of Authority in the *Community Rule*." Pages 61–90 in *The Process of Authority: The Dynamics in Transmission and Reception of Canonical Texts*. Edited by Jan Dušek and Jan Roskovec. DCLS 27. Berlin: de Gruyter.

Hempel, Charlotte. 1993. "Comments on the Translation of 4QS^d I, 1." *JJS* 44:127–28.

———. 2003a. "The Community and Its Rivals according to the Community Rule from Caves 1 and 4." *RevQ* 21:47–81.

———. 2003b. "Interpretative Authority in the Community Rule Tradition." *DSD* 10:58–80.

———. 2006. "The Literary Development of the S Tradition—A New Paradigm." *RevQ* 22:389–401.

———. 2009. "Vielgestaltigkeit und Verbindlichkeit: Serekh ha-Yachad in Qumran." Pages 101–20 in *Qumran und der biblische Kanon*. Edited by Jörg Frey and Michael Becker. Neukirchen-Vluyn: Neukirchener Verlag.

———. 2010. "The Treatise on the Two Spirits and the Literary History of the Rule of the Community." Pages 102–20 in *Dualism in Qumran*. Edited by Géza G. Xeravits. LSTS 76. London: T&T Clark.

———. 2013. *The Qumran Rule Texts in Context: Collected Studies*. TSAJ 154. Tübingen: Mohr Siebeck.

———. 2015. "The Long Text of Serekh as Crisis Literature." *RevQ* 27:3–24.

———. 2019. "Rules." Pages 405–12 in *T&T Clark Companion to the Dead Sea Scrolls*. Edited by George J. Brooke and Charlotte Hempel. London: T&T Clark.

Hendel, Ronald. 2008. "The Oxford Hebrew Bible: Prologue to a New Critical Edition." *VT* 58:324–51.

———. 2016. *Steps to a New Edition of the Hebrew Bible*. TCSt 10. Atlanta: SBL Press.

Hultgren, Stephen. 2019. "Serekh ha-Yahad." Pages 344–46 in *T&T Clark Companion to the Dead Sea Scrolls*. Edited by George J. Brooke and Charlotte Hempel. London: T&T Clark.

Jokiranta, Jutta. 2016. "What Is 'Serekh ha-Yahad (S)'? Thinking about Ancient Manuscripts as Information Processing." Pages 611–35 in *Sibyls, Scriptures, and Scrolls: John Collins at Seventy*. Edited by Joel Baden, Hindy Najman, and Eibert J. C. Tigchelaar. JSJSup 175. Leiden: Brill.

Jokiranta, Jutta, and Hanna Vanonen. 2015. "Multiple Copies of Rule Texts or Multiple Rule Texts?" Pages 11–60 in *Crossing Imaginary Boundaries: The Dead Sea Scrolls in the Context of Second Temple Judaism*. Edited by Mika S. Pajunen and Hanna Tervanotko. Publications of the Finnish Exegetical Society 108. Helsinki: Finnish Exegetical Society.

Knibb, Michael A. 1987. *The Qumran Community*. CCWJCW 2. Cambridge: Cambridge University Press.

———. 2000. "Rule of the Community." Pages in 793–97 in vol. 2 of *Encyclopedia of the Dead Sea Scrolls*. Edited by Lawrence H. Schiffman and James C. VanderKam. 2 vols. Oxford: Oxford University Press.

Kratz, Reinhard G. 2011. "Der *Penal Code* und das Verhältnis von *Serekh Ha-Yachad* (S) und Damaskusschrift (D)." *RevQ* 25:199–227.

Leaney, A. R. C. 1966. *The Rule of Qumran and Its Meaning: Introduction, Translation and Commentary*. London: SCM.

Lucas, Alec J. 2010. "Scripture Citations as an Internal Redactional Control: 1QS 5:1–20a and Its 4Q Parallels." *DSD* 17:30–52.

Martin, Malachi. 1958. *The Scribal Character of the Dead Sea Scrolls*. 2 vols. Leuven: Publications universitaires.

Metso, Sarianna. 1998. "Constitutional Rules at Qumran." Pages 186–210 in *The Dead Sea Scrolls after Fifty Years: A Comprehensive Assessment*. Edited by Peter W. Flint and James C. VanderKam. Leiden: Brill.

———. 1999. "In Search of the *Sitz im Leben* of the Community Rule." Pages 306–15 in *The Provo International Conference on the Dead Sea Scrolls: Technological Innovations, New Texts, and Reformulated Issues*. Edited by Donald W. Parry and Eugene Ulrich. STDJ 30. Leiden: Brill.

———. 2004. "Methodological Problems in Reconstructing History from Qumran Rule Texts." *DSD* 11:315–35.

———. 2005. "Whom Does the Term *Yaḥad* Identify?" Pages 213–35 in *Biblical Traditions in Transmission: Essays in Honour of Michael A. Knibb*. Edited by Charlotte Hempel and Judith Lieu. JSJSup 111. Leiden: Brill.

———. 2006. "Creating Community Halakha." Pages 279–301 in *Studies in the Hebrew Bible, Qumran, and the Septuagint Presented to Eugene Ulrich*. Edited by Peter W. Flint, Emanuel Tov, and James C. VanderKam. VTSup 101. Leiden: Brill.

———. 2007. *The Serekh Texts*. CQS 9; LSTS 62. London: T&T Clark.

———. 2009. "Problems in Reconstructing the Organizational Chart of the Essenes." *DSD* 16:388–415.

———. 2017. "The Burden of Proof: Challenges in Explaining the Redactional Evidence of the Treatise on the Two Spirits." Pages 151–61 in *Insights into Editing in the Hebrew Bible and Ancient Near East*. Edited by Reinhard Müller, Juha Pakkala, and Bas ter Haar Romeny. CBET 84. Leuven: Peeters.

Metso, Sarianna, and James Tucker. 2017. "The Changing Landscape of Editing Ancient Jewish Texts." Pages 269–87 in *Reading the Bible in Ancient Traditions and Modern Editions: Studies in Memory of Peter W. Flint*. Edited by Andrew B. Perrin, Kyung S. Baek, and Daniel K. Falk. EJL 47. Atlanta: SBL Press.

Milik, Józef T. 1956. "Le travail d'édition des fragments manuscrits de Qumran." *RB* 63:4–67.

———. 1960. "Textes des variantes des dix manuscrits de la Règle de la Communauté trouvés dans la Grotte 4: Recension de P. Wernberg-Moeller, The Manual of Discipline." *RB* 67:410–16.

———. 1972. "Milkî-ṣedeq et Milkî-Rešaʿ dans les anciens écrits juifs et chrétiens." *JJS* 23:95–144.

———. 1976. *The Books of Enoch*. Oxford: Clarendon.

———. 1977. "Numérotation des feuilles des rouleaux dans le scriptorium de Qumrân (Planches X et XI)." *Semitica* 27:75–81.

Murphy-O'Connor, Jérôme. 1969. "La genèse littéraire de la Règle de la Communauté." *RB* 76:528–49.

Novick, Tzvi. 2013. "Column Five of the Community Rule: Two Notes." *RevQ* 26:115–25.

Puech, Émile. 1979. "Remarques sur l'écriture de 1QS VII–VIII." *RevQ* 10:35–43.

Qimron, Elisha. 1986 *The Hebrew of the Dead Sea Scrolls*. Harvard Semitic Studies 29. Atlanta: Scholars Press.

Reymond, Eric D. 2014. *Qumran Hebrew: An Overview of Orthography, Phonology, and Morphology*. RBS 76. Atlanta: SBL Press.

Schofield, Alison. 2008. "Rereading S: A New Model of Textual Development in Light of the Cave 4 Serekh Copies." *DSD* 15:96–120.

———. 2009. *From Qumran to the Yaḥad: A New Paradigm of Textual Development for The Community Rule*. STDJ 77. Leiden: Brill.

Tigchelaar, Eibert J. C. 2000. "A Newly Identified 11QSerekh Ha-Yaḥad Fragment (11Q29)?" Pages 285–92 in *The Dead Sea Scrolls: Fifty Years after Their Discovery. Proceedings of the Jerusalem Congress, July 20–25, 1997*. Edited by Lawrence H. Schiffman, Emanuel Tov, and James C. VanderKam. Jerusalem: Israel Exploration Society in cooperation with the Shrine of the Book, Israel Museum.

———. 2004. "'These Are the Names of the Spirits of…': A Preliminary Edition of 4QCatalogue of Spirits (4Q230) and New Manuscript Evidence for the Two Spirits Treatise (4Q257 and 1Q29a)." *RevQ* 21:529–47.

———. 2007. "Catalogue of Spirits, Liturgical Manuscript with Angelological Content, Incantation? Reflections on the Character of a Fragment from Qumran (4Q230 1), With Appendix: Edition of the Fragments of IAA #114." Pages 133–46 in *A Kind of Magic: Understanding Magic in the New Testament and Its Religious Environment*. Edited by Michael Labahn and Bert Jan Lietaert Peerbolte. LNTS 306. New York: T&T Clark.

Tov, Emanuel. 2004. *Scribal Practices and Approaches Reflected in the Texts Found in the Judean Desert*. STDJ 54. Leiden: Brill.

Tucker, James M. 2019. "From Ink Traces to Ideology: A Reassessment of 4Q256 (4QSerekh ha-Yaḥad[b]) Frgs. 5a–b and 1QS 6:16–17." Pages 185–206 in *Law, Literature, and Society in Legal Texts from Qumran: Papers from the Ninth Meeting of the International Organization for Qumran Studies, Leuven 2016*. Edited by Jutta Jokiranta and Molly Zahn. STDJ 128. Leiden: Brill.

Ulrich, Eugene. 1999. *The Dead Sea Scrolls and the Origins of the Bible*. Studies in the Dead Sea Scrolls and Related Literature. Leiden: Brill; Grand Rapids: Eerdmans.

———. 2002. "The Absence of 'Sectarian Variants' in the Jewish Scriptural Scrolls Found at Qumran." Pages 179–95 in *The Bible as Book: The Hebrew Bible and the Judaean Desert Discoveries*. Edited by Edward D. Herbert and Emanuel Tov. London: The British Library and Oak Knoll Press.

———. 2010. "The Evolutionary Production and Transmission of the Scriptural Books." Pages 209–25 in *The Dead Sea Scrolls: Transmission of Traditions and Production of Texts*. Edited by Sarianna Metso, Hindy Najman, and Eileen Schuller. STDJ 92. Leiden: Brill.

———. 2015. *The Dead Sea Scrolls and the Developmental Composition of the Bible*. VTSup 169. Leiden: Brill.

VanderKam, James C. 1999. "The Judean Desert and the Community of the Dead Sea Scrolls." Pages 159–71 in *Antikes Judentum und Frühes Christentum: Festschrift für Hartmut Stegemann zum 65. Geburtstag*. Edited by Bernd Kollmann, Wolfgang Reinbold, and Annette Steudel. BZNW 97. Berlin: de Gruyter.

Vermes, Geza. 1991. "Preliminary Remarks on Unpublished Fragments of the Community Rule from Qumran Cave 4." *JJS* 42:250–55.

———. 1996. "The Leadership of the Qumran Community: Sons of Zadok – Priests - Congregation." Pages 375–84 in Volume 1 of *Geschichte – Tradition – Reflexion: Festschrift für Martin Hengel zum 70. Geburtstag*. Edited by Hubert Cancik, Hermann Lichtenberger, and Peter Schäfer. 3 vols. Tübingen: Mohr Siebeck.

Hebrew Text and English Translation

Column I

1 [ל   [שים לח]יו ⸢ספר ס⸣רך היחד לדרוש

2 אל ב[כול ל]ב̇ ובכו̇ל נפש ⸣ לעשות הטוב והישר לפניו כאשר

3 צוה ביד מושה וביד כול עבדיו הנביאים ולאהוב כול

4 אשר בחר ולשנוא את כול אשר מאס לרחוק מכול רע

5 ולדבוק בכול מעשי טוב ולעשות אמת וצדקה ומשפט

6 בארץ ולוא ללכת עוד בשרירות לב אשמה ועיני זנות

7 לעשות כול רע ולהבי את כול הנדבים לעשות חוקי אל

8 בברית חסד להי̇חד בעצת אל ולהתהלב̇ לפניו תמים כול

9 הנגלות למועדי תעודותם ולאהוב כול בני אור איש

10 כגורלו בעצת אל ולשנוא כול בני חושך איש כאשמתו

11 בנקמ̇ת אל וכול הנדבים לאמתו יביאו כול דעתם וכוחם

12 והונם ביחד אל לברר דעתם באמת חוקי אל וכוחם לתכן

13 כתם דרכיו וכול הונם כעצת צדקו ולוא לצעוד בכול אחד

14 מכול דברי אל בקציהם ולוא לקדם עתיהם ולוא להתאחר

15 מכול מועדיהם ולוא לסור מחוקי אמתו ללכת ימין ושמאול

16 וכול הבאים בסרכ היחד יעבורו בברית <> לפני אל לעשות

17 ככול אשר צוה ולוא לשוב מאחרי מכול פחד ואימה ומצרף

18 נוסוים בממשלת בליעל ובעוברם בברית יהיו הכוהנים

19 והלויים מברכים את אל ישועות ואת כול מעשי אמתו וכול

20 העוברים בברית אומרים אחריהם אמן אמן

⸗

21 *vacat* והכוהנים מספרים את צדקות אל במעשי גבורתום

22 ומשמיעים כול חסדי רחמים על ישראל והלויים מספרים

1QS 1:1–26 — 4QS^a 1 1–6 (par. 1QS 1:1–5); 4QS^c I, 1–2 (par. 1QS 1:2–3); 4QS^b I, 9 (1QS 1:10); 4QS^b II, 1–9 (par. 1QS 1:15–19; 21–23)

1:1 None of the manuscripts of S has preserved the opening words of the document in their entirety. For possible reconstructions, see Metso 1997, 111–12. ‖ ספר סרכ 4QS^a; the text is only partially preserved in 1QS with [רֿך̇   ]. ‖ **2** [בֿוכלֿוב̇ 4QS^c and לעשוֿת̇[ול נפש ובכ 4QS^a; not preserved in 1QS. This partially reconstructed phrase בכל לב ובכל נפש also occurs in 1QS 5:8–9 (par. 4QS^d I, 6). ‖ **16** In יעבורו 1QS, the scribe first wrote the word with an א, then corrected it to ע. Alexander and Vermes (1998, 48) read a superscript *aleph* at the end of the word in 4QS^b, but color photograph B-366910 clearly shows that what they probably take as a leg of an *aleph* is, in fact, a shadow cast by the edge of the fragment. ‖ In 1QS, the letter removed in לפני< > was possibly an א. ‖ **18** It appears that in נוסוים 1QS the scribe initially skipped ס and wrote נו instead but corrected his mistake by writing ס on top of both letters and then continued וים. ‖ **19** The scribe seems to have initially written singular מעשה but then corrected it to plural construct מעשי. ‖ **21** For -ום ending in גבורתום, see רוחום in 1QS 5:21 and 9:14, where *qameṣ* is phonologically represented by ו. See Qimron 1986, §200.143.

Column I

1. For […] for his life, the book of the rule of the community. They shall seek
2. God wi[th a whole he]art and soul; they shall do what is good and right before him in accordance with that which
3. he commanded through Moses and through all his servants the prophets; they shall love all
4. that he has chosen and hate all that he has rejected; they shall keep away from all evil
5. and cling to all good works; they shall practice truth, righteousness, and justice
6. in the land and not continue walking in the stubbornness of a guilty heart and of lustful eyes,
7. committing all evil. They shall admit into the covenant of love all those who willingly offer themselves to observe the statutes of God,
8. so that they may be joined to the counsel of God and may walk perfectly before him in accordance with all
9. the things that have been revealed at the times appointed for their revelation and so that they may love all the sons of light, each
10. according to his lot in the plan of God, and may hate all the sons of darkness, each according to his guilt
11. in the vengeance of God. And all those who willingly offer themselves to his truth shall bring all their knowledge, their abilities,
12. and their wealth into the community of God, that they may purify their knowledge in the truth of the statutes of God and may order their abilities
13. according to his perfect ways and all their wealth according to his righteous counsel. They shall not depart from any one
14. of all the commandments of God concerning their times; they shall not anticipate their appointed times or be behind
15. in any of their feasts. They shall not turn from his true statutes to go to the right or the left.
16. All those who join the order of the community shall enter into a covenant before God to do
17. all that he has commanded and not to turn back from following him through any fear or terror or trial
18. that takes place during the reign of Belial. When they enter into the covenant, the priests and the Levites shall
19. bless the God of salvation and all the deeds of his faithfulness, and all
20. those who are entering into the covenant say after them, "Amen, Amen!"

21. The priests recount the righteous acts of God manifested in his mighty deeds
22. and proclaim all his gracious acts of love toward Israel. And the Levites recount

---

The translation of columns I–IX is by Michael A. Knibb, slightly adapted in light of the Cave 4 evidence. The translation of columns X–XI is by Sarianna Metso.

23 את עוונות בני ישראל וכול פשעי אשמתם וחטאתם בממשלת

24 בליעל [וכו]ל֯ העוברים בברית מודים אחריהם לאמור נעווינו

25 פ֯[ש֯ע֯נ֯ו֯] [חט]א֯נו הרשענו אנו [וא]ב֯ותינו מלפנינו ב<ה>֯לכתנו

26 [משפטו בנו ובאבותי֯נ֯ו֯]   [ ]ל֯[ ]   [אמת וצדיק֯]

Column II

1 ורחמי חסדו ג֯מל עלינו מעולם ועד עולם vacat והכוהנים מברכים את כול

2 אנשי גורל אל ההולכים תמים בכול דרכיו ואומרים יברככה בכול

3 טוב וישמורכה מכול רע יאר לבכה בשכל חיים ויחונכה בדעת עולמים

4 וישא פני חסדיו֯⌐ ⌐לכה לשלום עולמים vacat והלויים מקללים את⌐ ⌐כול אנשי

5 גורל בליעל וענו ואמרו ארור אתה בכול מעשי֯⌐ ⌐רשע אשמתכה יתנכה

6 אל זעוה ביד כול נוקמי נקם ויפקוד אחריכה כלה֯ ⌐ביד כול משלמי

7 גמולים ארור אתה לאין רחמים֯ כחושך מעשיכה וזעום אתה

8 באפלת אש עולמים לוא יחונכה אל בקוראכה ולוא יסלח לכפר עווניך

9 ישא פני אפו לנקמתכה ולוא יהיה לכה שלום בפי כול אוחזי אבות

10 וכול העוברים בברית אומרים אחר המברכים והמקללים אמן אמן

11 vacat והוסיפו הכוהנים והלויים ואמרו ארור בגלולי לבו לעבור

12 הבא בברית הזות ומכשול עוונו ישים לפניו להסוג בו והיה

13 בשומעו את⌐ ⌐דברי הברית הזות יתברכ֯ בלבבו לאמור שלום יהי⌐ ⌐לי

14 כיא בשרירות לבי אלכ֯ ונספתה רוחו הצמאה עם הרווה לאין

15 סליחה אף אל וקנאת משפטיו יבערו בו לכלת עולמים ידבקו בו כול

16 אלות הברית הזות ויבדילהו אל לרעה ונכרת מתוך כול בני אור בהסוגו

17 מאחרי⌐ ⌐אל בגלוליו ומכשול עוונו יתן גורלו בתוך ארורי עולמים

18 vacat וכול באי הברית יענו ואמרו אחריהם אמן אמן

19 vacat ככה יעשו שנה בשנה כול יומי ממשלת בליעל הכוהנים יעבורו

1QS 2:1–26 — 4QS^b II, 9–13 (par. 1QS 2:4–5); 5QS 1 I, 2–6 (par. 1QS 2:4–7) 4QS^c II, 1–8 (par. 1QS 2:4–11); 4QS^b III, 1–4 (par. 1QS 2:6–11); 5QS 1 II, 1–3 (par. 1QS 2:12–14); 4QS^c III, 1 (par. 1QS 2:26)

2:4 Word space in חסדיו⌐ ⌐לכה not extant in 1QS. ‖ Word space in את כול is extant in 4QS^c but not in 1QS. ‖ **5** Word space in מעשי֯⌐ ⌐רשע not extant in 1QS. ‖ **6** Word space in כלה ביד is extant in 4QS^b but not in 1QS. ‖ **7** 1QS [כחושך בחושך 4QS^b ‖ **8** עווניך 1QS] ו[ע]נכה 4QS^b; [ענ]ונכה 4QS^c ‖ **11** In 1QS, the last letter of the line is clearly a *resh*, but some commentators (e.g., Knibb 1987, 83 and 87; Qimron and Charlesworth 1994b, 11 n. 31) suggest an emendation and read לעבוד. ‖ **12** In 1QS, although להסוג seems to be the more probable reading, להמוג is also possible. Cf. the shape of *samek* in חסדים in 1QS 4:5. ‖ **13** Word space in את⌐ ⌐דברי not extant in 1QS. ‖ Word space in יהי⌐ ⌐לי not extant in 1QS. ‖ **17** Word space in מאחרי⌐ ⌐אל not extant in 1QS.

23 the iniquities of the children of Israel and all their guilty transgressions and their sins during the reign
24 of Belial. [And all] those who are entering into the covenant confess after them and say: "We have committed iniquity
25 [and tr]ansgressed, we have [sin]ned and acted wickedly, we [and] our [fath]ers before us, in that we have walked
26 […] of truth and righteousness […] his judgment upon us and upon our fathers,

Column II

1 but he has bestowed his loving grace upon us from everlasting to everlasting." And the priests bless all
2 the men of the lot of God who walk perfectly in all his ways and say: "May he bless you with all
3 good and keep you from all evil. May he enlighten your heart with understanding of life and graciously bestow upon you knowledge of eternity.
4 May he lift up the face of his mercy upon you in eternal peace." And the Levites curse all the men of the lot
5 of Belial and answer and say: "Cursed be you for all your guilty deeds of wickedness. May God give you up
6 to terror at the hand of all who take vengeance, and may he visit destruction upon you at the hand of all who exact
7 retribution. Cursed be you without mercy for the darkness of your deeds, and damned be you
8 in the gloom of everlasting fire. May God not show mercy to you when you call or forgive you by making expiation for your iniquities.
9 May he lift up the face of his anger to take vengeance on you, and may there be no peace for you in the mouth of all who make intercession."
10 And all those who are entering into the covenant say after those who bless and those who curse, "Amen, Amen!"

ך

11 And the priests and the Levites shall continue and say: "Cursed for the idols of his heart by which he transgresses
12 be the one who enters into this covenant while placing before himself the stumbling block of his iniquity so that he backslides because of it. When
13 he hears the terms of this covenant, he will bless himself in his heart and say, 'May there be peace for me,
14 even though I walk in the stubbornness of my heart.' But his spirit shall be destroyed, the dry with the moist, without
15 forgiveness. May the anger of God and the wrath of his judgments burn upon him for everlasting destruction. May all
16 the curses of this covenant cling to him. May God set him apart for evil, and may he be cut off from all the sons of light because of his backsliding
17 from God through his idols and the stumbling block of his iniquity. May he assign his lot among those who are cursed forever."
18 And all those who are entering the covenant answer and say after them, "Amen, Amen!"

ך

19 Thus they shall do every year, as long as the reign of Belial lasts. The priests shall enter

20 ברשונה בסרך לפי רוחותם זה אחר זה והלויים יעבורו אחריהם
21 וכול העם <> יעבורו בשלישית בסרכ זה אחר זה לאלפים ומאות
22 וחמשים ועשרות לדעת כול איש ישראל איש בית מעמדו ביחד אל
23 לעצת עולמים ולוא ישפל איש מבית מֿעמדו ולוא ירום ממקום גורלו
24 כיא הכול יהיו ביחד אמת וענות טוב וֹאהבת חסד ומחשבת צדק
25 אֹֿיש לרעהו בעצת קודש ובני סוד עולמים וכול המואס לבוא
26 [בברית א]ל ללכת בשרירות לבו לוא ֿי[   ]ֿי[י]ֿחד אמתו כיא געלה

Column III

1 נפשו ביסורי דעת משפטי צדק לוא חזק למשוֹב ֿח[   ]ֿיו ועם ישרים לוא יתחשב
2 ודעתו וכוחו והונו לוא יבֿיאֿו בעצת יחד כיא בסֿאון רשע מחרשו וגֿ[א]ֿולים
3 בשובתו ולוא יצדק במתור שרירות לבו וחושכ יביט לדרכי אור בעין תמימים
4 לוא יתחשב לוא יזכה בכפורים ולוא יטהר במי נדה ולוא יתקדש בימים
5 ונהרות ולוא יטהר בכול מי רחץ טמא טמא יהיה כול יומי מאוסו במשפטי
6 אל לבלתי התיסר ביחד עצתו כיא ברוח עצת אמת אל דרכי איש יכופרו כול
7 עוונותו להביט באור החיים וברוח קדושה ליחד באמתו יטהר מכול
8 עוונותו וברוח יושר וענוה תכופר חטתו ובענות נפשו לכול חוקי אל יטהר
9 בשרו להזות במי נדה ולהתקדש במי דוכֿיֿ ויהכין פעמיו להלכת תמים
10 בכול דרכי אל כאשר צוה למועדי תעודתיו ולוא לסור ימין ושמאול ואין
11 לצעוד על אחד מכול דבריו אז ירצה בכפורי ניחוח לפני אל והיתה לו לברית
12 יחד עולמים   vacat

13 vacat למשכיל להבין וללמד את כול בני אור בתולדות כול בני איש
14 לכול מיני רוחותם באותותם למעשיהם בדורותם ולפקודת נגיעיהם עם

1QS 3:1–26 — 4QS[c] III, 1–14 (par. 1QS 3:1–10); 4QS[h] 1 1–4 (par. 1QS 3:4–5); 4QS[a] 2 1–9 (1QS 3:7–12)

2:26 Reconstruction of [בברית א]ל is based on 1QS 5:8 and 10:10. ‖ 4QS[c] preserves *yod* of the next word after לוא. ‖ **3:1** The reading למשוֹב is equally uncertain in 4QS[c] (לֿמֿשׁוֹב), and למשׁיב is an alternative, plausible reading in both 1QS and 4QS[c]. Because of the uncertainty of the reading, a variant between the manuscripts is possible. ‖ *Ḥet* of חיו, while only partially preserved in 1QS (חֿיו), is fully extant in 4QS[c]. ‖ **2** In both 1QS and 4QS[c], either a *qal* or *hiphil* is possible to read in יביאו, and a variant between the manuscripts is possible. ‖ The superscript *aleph* in 1QS וגֿאֿולים is preserved partially in 4QS[c] וגֿאֿ]וֿלֿ[ים ‖ **5** 1QS רחץ] רחיצה 4QS[h] ‖ **7** 1QS קדושה] קודשו 4QS[a] ‖ **8** 1QS עוונתו] עונתו 4QS[a]. Alexander and Vermes (1998) read עוונֿתו 4QS[a], but color photograph B-511794 clearly shows that there is no *vav* between *nun* and *taw*. ‖ יושר] ישר 4QS[a] ‖ Read חטאתו as חטתו. ‖ **9** 1QS במי] [בכול מי 4QS[a] ‖ 1QS דוכֿיֿ ויהכין פעמיו] דוכי יבין]ֿ 4QS[a]. Alexander and Vermes as well as Qimron read [עמיו יהכין] וֿפֿ[דוכי in 4QS[a], but the letter preceding the lacuna does not appear to be a *pe*. It is more likely a *kaph*; for similar phraseology, see 1QS 11:10 and esp. 11:13. ‖ 1QS להלכת] להלכ 4QS[a] ‖ **10** 1QS תעודתו] תעודתיו 1QS ‖ **11** 1QS לפני אל] > 4QS[a]

20 into the order first, one after another according to their spiritual status. And the Levites shall enter after them.
21 And thirdly all the people shall enter into the order, one after another, by thousands, hundreds,
22 fifties, and tens, so that every man of Israel may know his own position in the community of God
23 according to the eternal plan. No man shall move down from his position or move up from his allotted place.
24 For they shall all be in a community of truth, virtuous humility, kindly love, and right intention
25 toward one another in a holy council, and they shall all be members of an eternal fellowship. No one who refuses to enter
26 [into the covenant of Go]d so that he may walk in the stubbornness of his heart [shall ... the comm]unity of his truth, for

Column III

1 his soul has spurned the disciplines involved in the knowledge of the precepts of righteousness; he has not devoted himself to the conversion of his life, and with the upright he shall not be counted.
2 His knowledge, his abilities, and his wealth shall not be brought into the council of the community, for he plows with wicked step, and defilement
3 accompanies his conversion. He shall not be justified when he follows the stubbornness of his heart, for he regards darkness as the ways of light. In the spring of the perfect
4 he shall not be counted. He shall not be made clean by atonement, or purified by waters for purification, or made holy by seas
5 and rivers, or purified by any water for washing. Unclean, unclean shall he be as long as he rejects the precepts
6 of God by refusing to discipline himself in the community of his counsel. For it is through a spirit of true counsel with regard to the ways of man that all
7 his iniquities shall be wiped out so that he may look on the light of life. It is through a holy spirit uniting him to his truth that he shall be purified from all
8 his iniquities. It is through a spirit of uprightness and humility that his sin shall be wiped out. And it is through the submission of his soul to all the statutes of God
9 that his flesh shall be purified, by being sprinkled with waters for purification and made holy by waters for cleansing. Let him, therefore, order his steps that he may walk perfectly
10 in all the ways of God in accordance with that which he commanded at the times (when he made known) his decrees, without turning to the right or left and without
11 going against any one of all his commandments. Then he will be accepted through soothing atonement before God, and it will be for him a covenant
12 of the eternal community.

╼

13 For the wise leader that he may instruct and teach all the sons of light about the history of all the sons of men
14 according to all the kinds of spirits revealed in the character of their deeds during their generations and according to their visitation of chastisement as well as

15 קצי שלומם מאל הדעות כול הויה ונהייה ולפני היותם הכין כול מחשבתם

16 ובהיותם לתעודותם כמחשבת כבודו ימלאו פעולתם ואין להשנות בידו

17 משפטי כול והואה יכלכלם בכול חפציהם והואה ברא אנוש לממשלת

18 תבל וישם לו שתי רוחות להתהלכ בם עד מועד פקודתו הנה רוחות

19 האמת והעול במע͏ן אור תולדות האמת וממקור חושכ תולדות העול

20 ביד שר אורים ממשלת כול בני צדק בדרכי אור יתהלכו וביד מלאך

21 חושך כול ממשלת בני עול ובדרכי חושך יתהלכו ובמלאך חושך תעות

22 כול בני צדק וכול חטאתם ועוונותם ואשמתם ופשעי מעשיהם בממשלתו

23 לפי͏ ⌐רזי¬ אל עד קצו וכול נגועיהם ומועדי צרותם בממשלת משטמתו

24 וכול͏ ⌐רוחי¬ גורלו להכשיל בני אור ואל ישראל ומלאכ אמתו עזר לכול

25 בני אור והואה ברא רוחות אור וחושך ועליהון יסד כול מעשה

26 [וע]ל͏ דרכ[י]הן כול עבודה ⌐ ¬ אחת אהב אל לכול

Column IV

1 [מו]עדי עולמים ובכול עלילותיה ירצה לעד אחת תעב סודה וכול דרכיה שנא לנצח

2 vacat ואלה דרכיהן בתבל להאיר בלבב איש ולישר לפניו כול דרכי צדק אמת ולפחד לבבו במשפטי

3 אל ורוח ענוה ואורכ אפים ורוב רחמים וטוב עולמים ושכל ובינה וחכמת גבורה מאמנת בכול

4 מעשי אל ונשענת ברוב חסדו ורוח דעת בכול מחשבת מעשה וקנאת משפטי צדק ומחשבת

5 קודש ביצר סמוכ ורוב חסדים על͏ ⌐כול¬ בני אמת וטהרת כבוד מתעב̇ת̇ כול גלולי נדה והצנע לכת

1QS 4:1–26 — 4QS^c V, 1–8 + *olim* 4Q502 frag. 16 (par. 1QS 4:4–10); 4QS^c V, 12–14 (par. 1QS 4:13–15); 4QS^c VI, 2–5 (par. 1QS 4:23–25)

3:15 Reading הויה with Qimron (2010, 215), presuming that the scribe made a play on words using a single root (היה and not הוה). ‖ **19** It is unclear whether the scribe intended to write מעון (dwelling) or מעין (spring). The stroke of *yod* seems quite long to support the reading of מעין, but, paralleled with מקור in this context, מעון seems more suited. Prov 25:26 similarly parallels מעין and מקור. See also 1QS 10:12, where *vav*/*yod* is similarly questionable. ‖ **22** 4QS^a frag. A may provide a loose parallel to 1QS 3:20–25, but too little is preserved of the fragment to make a definitive identification. Line 2 of 4QS^a frag. A (דרכי איש[) can be compared with 1QS 3:20, line 4 (איש ⌐בני¬ ⌐וכול רוחות¬[) with 1QS 3:24, and line 5 (חושכ [ ] °°אור ו[) with 1QS 3:25. See photo B-371754 frag. 4. If, in fact, a parallel, the form of 4QS^a is probably the earlier one. While 4QS^a line 4 uses the generic בני איש, in 1QS it is supplanted by a theologized בני אור in 3:24. ‖ In 1QS בממשלתו the last two letters have been written vertically in the margin. ‖ **23** Word space in לפי͏ ⌐רזי¬ not extant in 1QS. ‖ **24** Word space in וכול͏ ⌐רוחי¬ not extant in 1QS. ‖ **26** The fragmentary text in 1QS [וע]ל͏ דרכ[י]הן כול עבודה ועל דרכיהן [כו]ל͏ [ע]בֹ̇וֹדה likely contains a dittography, with the words ועל דרכיהן כול עבודה copied twice. In line 26, the ceiling brackets indicate the position of the deletion. ‖ **4:1** Qimron's reconstruction is probably correct in presuming that some letters preceded עדי, and his reconstruction of [מו]עדי is likely, especially since some traces of ink from the *vav* are extant. ‖ **5** Word space in על͏ ⌐כול¬ not extant in 1QS. ‖ מתעב̇ת̇ 4QS^c] מתעב 1QS. The reading of 4QS^c is preferable in the context.

15 their times of reward. From the God of knowledge comes everything that is and will be. Before they existed he fixed all their plans,
16 and when they come into existence they complete their work according to their instructions in accordance with his glorious plan and without changing anything. In his hand
17 are the laws for all things, and he sustains them in all their concerns. He created man to rule
18 all the world, and he assigned two spirits to him that he might walk by them until the appointed time of his visitation; they are the spirits

⇗

19 of truth and of injustice. From a spring of light come the generations of truth, and from a well of darkness the generations of injustice.
20 Control over all the sons of righteousness lies in the hand of the prince of lights, and they walk in the ways of light; complete control over the sons of injustice lies in the hand of the angel
21 of darkness, and they walk in the ways of darkness. It is through the angel of darkness that all the sons of righteousness go astray,
22 and all their sins, their iniquities, their guilt, and their deeds of transgression are under his control
23 in the mysteries of God until his time. All their afflictions and their times of distress are brought about by his rule of hatred,
24 and all the spirits of his lot make the sons of light stumble. But the God of Israel and his angel of truth help all
25 the sons of light. He created the spirits of light and of darkness, and upon them he founded every deed,
26 [and upon] their [ways] every work [...] God loves one for all

Column IV

1 times of eternity, and he delights in all its actions forever; the other, he loathes its counsel and hates all its ways forever.

⇗

2 These are their ways in the world: to enlighten the heart of man, to make level before him all the ways of true righteousness, and to instill in his heart reverence for the precepts
3 of God, a spirit of humility, patience, abundant compassion, eternal goodness, insight, understanding, strong wisdom that trusts in all
4 the deeds of God and relies on the abundance of his kindness, a spirit of his knowledge with regard to every plan of action, zeal for the precepts of righteousness, a holy purpose
5 with a constant mind, abundant kindness toward all the sons of truth, a glorious purity that loathes all the impure idols, circumspection

---

3:26 1QS contains a dittography: the words "and upon their ways every work" have been accidentally repeated. They have been deleted in the translation.

6 בערמת כול וחבא לאמת רזי דעת *vacat* אלה סודי רוח לבני אמֹת תבל ופקודת כול הולכי בה למרפא
7 ורוב שלום באורכ ימים ופרות זרע עם כול ברכות עד ושמחת עולמים בחיי נצח וכליל כבוד
8 עם מדת הדר באור עולמים *vacat*

9 *vacat* ולרוח עולה רחוב נפש ושפול ידים בעבודת צדק רשע ושקר גוה ורום לבב כחש ורמיה אכזרי
10 ורוב חנפ קצור אפים ורוב אולת וקנאת זדון מעשי תועבה ברוח זנות ודרכי נדה בעבודת טמאה
11 ולשון גדופים עורון עינים וכבוד אוזן קושי עורפ וכובוד לב ללכת בכול דרכי חושכ וערמת רוע ופקודת
12 כול הולכי בה לרוב נגוֹעים ביד כול מלאכי חבל לשחת עולמים באפ עברת אל נקמוֹת לזעות נצח וחרפת
13 עד עמֹ[ ]כלמת כלה באש מחשכים וכול קציהם לדורותם באבל יגון ורעת מרורים בהויֹות חושכ עד
14 כלותם לאין שרית ופליטה למו *vacat*

15 *vacat* באלה[ ]תולדות כול בני איש ובמפלגיהן ינחלו כול צבאותם לדורותם ובדרכיהן יתהלכו וכול פעולת
16 מעשיהם במפלגיהן לפי נחלת איש בין רוב למועט לכול קצי עולמים כיא אל שמן בד בבד עד קץ
17 אחרון ויתן איבת עולם בין מפלגותˢ תועבת אמת עלילות עולה ותועבת עולה כול דרכי אמת וקנאת
18 ריב על כול משפטיהן כיא לוא יחד יתהלכו ואל ברזי שכלו ובחכמת כבודו נתן קץ להיות עולה ובמועד
19 פקודה ישמידנה לעד ואז תצא לנצח אמת תבל כיא התגוללה בדרכי רשע בממשלת עולה עד
20 מועד משפט נחרצה ואז יברר אל באמתו כול מעשי גבר יזקק לו מבני איש להתם כול רוח עולה מתכמי
21 בשרו ולטהרו ברוח קודש מכול עלילות רשעה ויז עליו רוח אמת כמי נדה מכול תועבות שקר והתגולל
22 ברוח נדה להבין ישרים בדעת עליון וחכמת בני שמים להשכיל תמימי דרך כיא בם בחר אל לברית עולמים
23 ולהם כול כבוד אדם ואין עולה יהיה לבושת כול מעשי רמיה עד הנה יריבו רוחי אמת ועול בלבב גבר
24 יתהלכו בחכמה ואולת וכפי נחלת איש באמֹת וצדק וכן ישנא עולה וכירשתו בגורל עול ירשע בו וכן
25 יתעב אמת כיא בד בבד שמן אל עד קץ נחרצה ועשות חדשה והואה ידע פעולת מעשיהן לכול קצי
26 [   ]ןֹ וינחילן לבני איש לדעת טוב [   ]לֹ [ה]פֹיל גורלות לכול חי לפי רוחו ב[ ]○   מועד [ה]פֹקודה

4:6 The ḥet in וחבא has been redrawn. ‖ **11** For the unusual form וכובוד, see Reymond 2014, 183; Qimron 2018, 331 (E 2.5.1). ‖ **12** It is unclear whether the scribe first wrote אל נקמות (as in Ps 94:1) with taw as the last letter but then secondarily erased the vav preceding it with the intention of reading the last letter as a he, i.e., נקמה. A small speck of the left tick of the vav is clearly visible, as is the bottom of the vertical stroke. Alternatively, the intended text was אל נקמות, and the scribe made no erasure, but rather the surface of the leather later slit, effectively erasing the vav and posing the question of the interpretation of the last letter. ‖ **13** Word space in כלמת ⌐עמ not extant in 1QS. ‖ **15** Word space in תולדות ⌐באלה not extant in 1QS. ‖ **26** Reconstruction on the basis of 1QS 3:18.

6 linked to discernment in all things, and concealment of the truth of the mysteries of knowledge. These are the counsels of the spirit for the sons of truth in the world. The visitation of all those who walk in it will be healing,
7 abundant peace with long life, fruitfulness with every everlasting blessing, eternal joy with life forever, and a crown of glory
8 with a garment of honor in eternal light.

9 To the spirit of injustice belong greed, slackness in the service of righteousness, wickedness and falsehood, pride and haughtiness, lying and deceit, cruelty
10 and great hypocrisy, impatience and abundant folly, zeal for insolence, abominable deeds committed in the spirit of lust, impure ways in the service of uncleanness,
11 a blaspheming tongue, blind eyes, a deaf ear, a stiff neck, a stubborn heart causing a man to walk in all the ways of darkness, and an evil cunning. The visitation
12 of all those who walk in it will be abundant chastisements at the hand of all the destroying angels, eternal destruction brought about by the anger of the avenging wrath of God, perpetual terror, and everlasting shame
13 with the ignominy of destruction in the fires of darkness. And all the times of their generations (will be spent) in sorrowful mourning and bitter distress in the abysses of darkness until
14 they are destroyed without remnant or survivor for them.

15 The history of all the sons of men is constituted by these (two spirits): in their (two) classes all their hosts in their generations have an inheritance, and in their ways they walk. All the work
16 that they do (is carried out) in relation to their (two) classes, depending on whether a man's inheritance is great or small, for all the times of eternity. For God has established them in equal parts until the last time
17 and has put eternal enmity between their (two) classes. An abomination to truth are the actions of injustice, and an abomination to injustice are all the ways of truth; there is a fierce
18 struggle between all their principles, for they do not walk together. But God in his mysterious insight and glorious wisdom has assigned an end to the existence of injustice, and at the appointed time
19 of the visitation he will destroy it forever. Then truth will appear in the world forever, for it has defiled itself in the ways of wickedness during the reign of injustice until
20 the time decreed for judgment. Then God will purify by his truth all the deeds of man and will refine for himself the frame of man, removing all spirit of injustice from within
21 his flesh, and purifying him by the spirit of holiness from every wicked action. And he will sprinkle upon him the spirit of truth like waters for purification (to remove) all the abominations of falsehood (in which) he has defiled himself
22 through the spirit of impurity, so that the upright may have understanding in the knowledge of the Most High, and the perfect of way insight into the wisdom of the sons of heaven. For it is they whom God has chosen for the eternal covenant,
23 and to them shall all the glory of Adam belong. There shall be no more injustice, and all the deeds of deceit shall be put to shame. Until now the spirits of truth and injustice struggle in the hearts of men,
24 and they walk in wisdom or in folly. According to a man's inheritance in truth and righteousness, so he hates injustice; and according to his share in the lot of injustice he acts wickedly through it and so
25 loathes truth. For God has established them in equal parts until the decreed end and the renewal. And he knows the work of their deeds for all the times
26 [of eternity], and he has given them as an inheritance to the sons of men that they may know good [..., and that he may deter]mine the fates of every living being according to the spirit within [him at the appointed time ... of the] visitation.

26 THE COMMUNITY RULE

Column V (1QS)		4QS^d I

vacat וזה הסרך לאנשי היחד המתנדבים לשוב מכול	1	מדרש למשכיל על אנשי התורה המתנדים להשיב	1
רע ולהחזיק בכול אשר צוה לרצונו להבדל מעדת		מכל רע ולהחזיק בכל אשר צוה	
אנשי העול להיות ליחד בתורה ובהון ומשיבים על פי	2	ול⌈ה⌉⌈בדל⌉ מעדת אנשי העול ולהיות יחד בתור⌈ה⌉	2
בני צדוק הכוהנים שומרי הברית ו⌈על⌉ ⌈פי רוב אנשי		ובהון ומשיבים על פי הרבים לכל דבר	
היחד המחזקים בברית על פיהם יצא⌉ ⌈תכון הגורל	3		
לכול דבר לתורה ולהון ולמשפט לעשות אמת יחד		לתורה ולהון ולעשות ענוה	3a
וענוה			
צדקה ומשפט ואהבת חסד והצנע לכת בכול	4	⌈ו⌉צדקה ומשפט ואהבת ⌈חסד וה⌉⌈צנע⌉	3b
דרכיהם אשר לוא ילך איש בשרירות לבו לתעות		לכת בכל דרכיהם	4
אחר לבבו		⌈אשר⌉ ⌈לא⌉ ילך איש בשרירות לבו	
ועיניהו ומחשבת יצרו ⌈כי אם⌉ למול ביחד עורלת	5	לתעות ⌈כי אם ליסד ⌉⌈מסד⌉ אמת לישראל	
יצר ועורף קשה ליסד מוסד אמת לישראל ליחד		ליחד לכל	
ברית			
עולם לכפר לכול המתנדבים לקודש באהרון ולבית	6	⌈המתנדב⌉ לקדש באהרן ובית אמת ל⌈ישראל	5
האמת בישראל והנלוים עליהם ליחד ולריב		והנלוי⌈ם⌉ ע⌈ל⌉י⌈ה⌉ם ליחד וכל הבא לעצת	
ולמשפט			
להרשיע כול עוברי חוק ואלה תכון דרכיהם על כול	7	⌈היח⌉⌈ד⌉ יקים על נפשו באסר ל⌈שוב א⌉⌈ל ת⌉⌈ורת	6
החוקים האלה בהאספם ליחד כול הבא לעצת היחד		מש⌈ה ב⌉⌈כל⌉ לב ובכל נפש כל הנגלה מן	

1QS 5:1–26 — 4QS^b IX, 1–13 (par. 1QS 5:1–20); 4QS^d I, 1–11 (par. 1QS 5:1–20); 4QS^d II, 1–5 (par. 1QS 5:21–26); 4QS^g 1 1–6 (par. 1QS 5:22–24)

5:1 In 4QS^d, there is a solitary *gimel* written in the top right margin. It is possible that the *gimel* signifies the third sheet in the manuscript. See Milik 1977, 75–81; Tov, 2004, 211. ‖ מדרש 4QS^d, [מדרש למשכיל על אנשי התורה 1QS] וזה הסרך לאנשי היחד ‖ להשיב 4QS^d [להשיב 1QS] לרצונו > 4QS^d ‖ להבדל 1QS] ולהבדל 4QS^b, ⌈למשכיל על⌉ 4QS^b ‖ המתנדים 4QS^d [המתנדבים 1QS] לשוב 4QS^d ‖ יח⌈ד⌉ 4QS^d [יחד 1QS ‖ ולהיות 4QS^d [להיות 1QS ‖ 2 ולבדל 4QS^d בני צדוק הכוהנים שומרי הברית ו⌈על⌉ ⌈פי רוב אנשי היחד המחזקים 2-3 [הרבים 4QS^{b, d}. Word space in ⌈ו⌉⌈על⌉ and ⌈תכון⌉ ⌈יצא⌉ not attested in 1QS. ‖ **3** In יחד in 1QS, the ink is smudged, and part of the surface of the leather appears damaged. It is unclear whether some letters were first erased and text was corrected or whether the smudged ink was created perhaps by a split tip of a quill. ‖ לעשות 4QS^d [> 1QS ‖ ולמשפט 1QS] > 4QS^d ‖ צדקה 1QS] ⌈ו⌉צדקה 4QS^d ‖ ולעשות ענוה 1QS] אמת יחד וענוה 4QS^d. **4** In 4QS^d (line 3b), the scribe first wrote לכל by mistake but then corrected it to לכת. ‖ In the copy text of 4QS^d, ⌈חסד וה⌉ is supplied by 4QS^b. ‖ In the copy text of 4QS^d, ⌈אשר⌉ is supplied by 4QS^b. ‖ **4–5** לתעות כי אם ליסד 4QS^d [לתעות אחר לבבו ועיניהו ומחשבת יצרו ⌈אם⌉ למול ביחד עורלת יצר ועורף קשה ליסד 1QS ‖ ⌈כי אם⌉ 4QS^d. The first letter of the word in 1QS, presumably a *yod*, has an unusual shape, so it is possible that a *kaph* in the source text had been misread. ‖ In the copy text of 4QS^d, ⌈מסד⌉ is supplied by 4QS^b. ‖ **5–6** ליחד ברית עולם לכפר לכול 1QS] > 4QS^d ‖ In the copy text of 4QS^d ובית אמת לישראל 4QS^b [ולבית האמת בישראל 1QS ‖ ⌈המתנדב⌉ 4QS^d [המתנדבים 1QS ‖ **6** ⌈המתנדב⌉ 4QS^d [לכל 1QS ליחד 4QS^d, some letters in והנלוי⌈ם⌉ ע⌈ל⌉י⌈ה⌉ם are supplied by 4QS^b. ‖ In 4QS^d (line 5), there is a possible *vacat* between ליחד and וכל. ‖ **6–7** ליחד ולריב ולמשפט להרשיע כול עוברי חוק ואלה תכון דרכיהם על כול החוקים האלה בהאספם ליחד כול 1QS] ליחד 4QS^d

Column V (1QS)

1. *This is the rule for* the men *of the community* who willingly offer themselves to *turn back* from all evil and to hold fast to all that he has commanded *as his will*. They shall separate themselves from the congregation

2. of the men of injustice to form a community in respect of the law and of wealth. They shall be answerable to the *sons of Zadok, the priests who keep the covenant, and to the multitude of the men*

3. *of the community who hold fast to the covenant; on their word the decision shall be taken* on any matter having to do with the law, with wealth, *or with justice. Together* they shall practice *truth and* humility,

4. righteousness and justice, kindly love and circumspection in all their ways. Let no man walk in the stubbornness of his heart so as to go astray *after his heart*

5. *and his eyes and the thought of his inclination! Rather, they shall circumcise in the community the foreskin of their inclination and of their stiff neck* that they may lay a foundation of truth for Israel, for the community *of the eternal covenant.*

6. *They shall make expiation* for all those who willingly offer themselves to holiness in Aaron and to the house of truth *in* Israel, and for those who join them in community. *In lawsuits and judgments*

7. they shall declare guilty all those who transgress the statute. These are their rules of conduct, according to all these statutes, when they are admitted to the community. Everyone who joins the council of the community

4QS^d I

1. *Instruction for the wise leader concerning the* men *of the law* who willingly offer themselves to *turn away* from all evil and to hold fast to all that he has commanded.

2. *And* they shall separate themselves from the congregation of the men of injustice *and* form a community in respect of the la[w] and of wealth. They shall be answerable to the *many* on any matter

3a. having to do with the law, with wealth, *and* they shall practice humility,

3b. *and* righteousness and justice, kindly love and circumspection in all their ways.

4. Let no man walk in the stubbornness of his heart so as to go astray.

Rather, they shall lay a foundation of truth for Israel, for the community, for all those

5. who willingly offer themselves to holiness in Aaron and to the house of truth *for* Israel and for those who join them in community.

And everyone who joins the council

6. of the community

28 THE COMMUNITY RULE

8	יבוא בברית אל לעיני כול המתנדבים ויקם על נפשו בשבועת אסר לשוב אל תורת מושה ככול אשר צוה בכול	
9	לב ובכול נפש לכול הנגלה ממנה לבני צדוק הכוהנים שומרי הברית ודורשי רצונו ולרוב אנשי בריתם	
7a		הת[ ]ל[ ] עצת אנש֯י היח֯ד להבדל מ[כו]ל אנ֯ש֯י העול
10	המתנדבים יחד לאמתו ולהתלכ ברצונו ואשר יקים בברית על נפשו להבדל מכול אנשי העול ההולכים	
11	בדרך הרשעה כיא לוא החשבו בבריתו כיא לוא בקשו ולוא דרשהו בחוקיהו לדעת הנסתרות אשר תעו	
12	בם לאשמה והנגלות עשו ביד רמה לעלות אף למשפט ולנקום נקם באלות ברית לעשות בם שפ<מ̇>טים	
7b		וא֯שר לא יגעו לטהרת אנשי
13	גדולים לכלת עולם לאין שרית vacat אל יבוא במים לגעת בטהרת אנשי הקודש כיא לוא יטהרו	
8aα		הקוד֯ש ואל יוכל אתו ב֯י֯ח֯ד
14	כי א֯ם שבו מרעתם כיא טמא בכול עוברי דברו ואשר לוא יוחד עמו בעבודתו ובהו<נ>ו פן ישיאנו	
15	עוון אשמה כיא ירחק ממנו בכול דבר כיא כן כתוב	
8aβ		ואשר ל[ו]א֯ [ישיב א]יש מאנשי
16	מכול דבר שקר תרחק ואשר לוא ישיב איש מאנשי היחד על פיהם לכול תורה ומשפט ואשר לוא יוכל	
8b		היחד על פיהם לכל
9		תורה ומשפט ואש֯ר לוא [ע֯ב̇ודה ואל] יואכל איש מאנשי הקדש
	מהונם כול ולוא ישתה ולוא יקח מידם כול מאומה	

5:7-8 ככול אשר צוה 4QS^b,d ‖ באסר 1QS] בשבועת אסר 4QS^d ‖ [היח̇]ד֯ יקים 4QS^d] היחד יבוא בברית אל לעיני כול המתנדבים ויקם 1QS ‖ **9** לכול 1QS] > 4QS^d ‖ In the copy text of 4QS^d, some letters in ל̇שוב א֯ל ת֯ו֯רת מש̇ה ב֯כ̇ל are supplied by 4QS^b. ‖ **9–10** 4QS^d ממנה לבני צדוק הכוהנים שומרי הברית ודורשי רצונו ולרוב אנשי בריתם המתנדבים יחד לאמתו ולהתלכ ברצונו ואשר יקים בברית על נפשו 1QS] מן הת [   ]ל̇[   ] עצת אנשי היחד 4QS^d. ‖ **10** In 4QS^d (lines 6–7), Alexander and Vermes (1998) are correct in positing a small piece attached to line 6 in PAM 43.244, not to line 6 but to the beginning of line 7. The letters preserved in the little fragment are הת. ‖ In the copy text of 4QS^d, some letters in להבדל מ֯ are supplied by 4QS^b. ‖ 4QS^b has preserved the *yod* in אנשי that in 4QS^d (line 7a) is preserved only partially. ‖ **10–13** ההולכים בדרך הרשעה כיא לוא החשבו בבריתו כיא לוא בקשו ולוא דרשהו בחוקיהו לדעת הנסתרות אשר תעו בם לאשמה והנגלות עשו ביד רמה לעלות אף למשפט ולנקום נקם באלות ברית לעשות בם שפ<מ̇>טים 1QS] > 4QS^b, d ‖ **12** לאשמה] לאששמה 1QS. The second *shin* of the word in 1QS is clearly an error. ‖ In שפ<מ̇>טים 1QS, erasure dots are visible above and below the erased *mem*. ‖ **13** לגעת בטהרת 1QS] וא֯שר לא יגעו לטהרת 4QS^d ‖ **13** In the copy text of 4QS^d, some letters in הקוד֯ש ואל יוכל אתו ב֯י֯ח֯ד are supplied by 4QS^b. ‖ **13–15** כיא לוא יטהר כיא א֯ם שבו מרעתם כיא טמא בכול עוברי דברו ואשר לוא יוחד עמו בעבודתו ובהו<נ>ו פן ישיאנו עוון אשמה כיא ירחק ממנו בכול דבר כיא כן כתוב 1QS] ואל יוכל אתו ב֯י֯ח֯ד 4QS^d ‖ **14** Word space in כי א֯ם not extant in 1QS. ‖ **15** Word space in כיא כן not extant in 1QS. ‖ **16** Word space in על פיהם not extant in 1QS. ‖ In the copy text of 4QS^d, תורה is supplied by 4QS^b. ‖ After ומשפט, 4QS^d contains an additional, partially preserved phrase ואשר לוא] ע֯ב̇ודה], which does not seem to have an equivalent in 1QS. Any reconstruction is uncertain. Alexander and Vermes (1998, 94) propose a reading similar to 1QS 5:14: וא֯ש]ר לוא יוחד עמו בהון וב[ע֯בודה. Qimron (2010, 219), on the

COLUMN V

8	*shall enter into the covenant of God in the presence of all those who willingly offer themselves.* He shall undertake by a *binding* oath to return to the law of Moses with all his		shall undertake by an oath to [return t]o the [l]aw of Mos[es] with all his heart and soul,
9	heart and soul, *following all that he has commanded* and in accordance with all that has been revealed from it *to the sons of Zadok, the priests who keep the covenant and seek his will, and to the multitude of the men of their covenant*		(to) all that has been revealed from
10	who together willingly offer themselves for his truth and to walk according to his will. He shall undertake *by the covenant* to separate himself from all the men of injustice *who walk*	7a	the [ ] *to* [ ] *council of the men* [*of*] *the community* [to separate himself from all the men] of injustice.
11	in the way of wickedness. For they are not counted in his covenant because they have not sought or consulted him about his statutes in order to know the hidden things in which they have guiltily gone astray,		
12	whereas with regard to the things revealed they have acted presumptuously, arousing anger for judgment and for taking vengeance by the curses of the covenant to bring upon themselves mighty acts of judgment		
13	leading to eternal destruction without a remnant. He shall not enter the waters in order to touch the purity of the men of holiness, *for men are not purified*	7b	*They shall not touch* the purity of the men
14	unless they turn from their evil, for he remains unclean among all the transgressors of his word. No one shall join with him with regard to his work or his wealth lest he burden him	8a	of holiness, *and he shall not eat with him in the community.*
15	with iniquity and guilt. But he shall keep away from him in everything, for thus it is written, "You shall keep away from everything false." No one of the men of the community shall answer		No one of the men of the community [shall answer]
16	to their authority with regard to any law or decision. No one shall eat *or drink anything of their property or take anything at all from their hand,*	8b	to their authority with regard to any
		9	law or decision and *tha*[*t*] *work. And* no one *from the men of holiness* shall eat

THE COMMUNITY RULE

17 אשר לוא במחיר כאשר כתוב חדלו לכם מן האדם
אשר נשמה באפו כיא במה נחשב הואה כיא

10 ל[ ] ○ולוא ישענו על [כל מע]שי ההבל
כי הבל כל אשר לא[ידעו]

18 כול אשר לוא נחשבו בבריתו להבדיל אותם ואת ⌈כול⌉
אשר להם ולוא ישען איש הקודש על כול מעשי

11 [את בריתו וכול מנאצ]י דברו להשמיד מתבל
ומעשיהם לנד⌈ה⌉ לפ[נ]⌈ו⌉[ ]ל[ ] [

19 הבל כיא הבל כול אשר לוא ידעו את בריתו וכול
מנאצי דברו ישמיד מתבל וכול מעשיהם לנדה

12]ם גוים ושבעות וחרמים ונדרים בפיהם [ ]
[ ]

20 לפניו וטמא בכול הונ<ו>ם וכיא יבוא בברית לעשות
ככול החוקים האלה ליחד לעדת קודש ודרשו

13]⌈דשל⌉[ ]ל[ ]○○○○○○[
[ל]

4QSᵈ II

1a ואת מעשיהם בתורה על פי בני
אהרון המתנדבים להקים

21 את⌈ ⌉⌈רוחום ביחד בין איש לרעהו לפי שכלו
ומעשיו בתורה על פי בני אהרון המתנדבים
ביחד להקים

1b את בריתו ולפקוד את כל חקיו אשר
צוה

22 את בריתו ולפקוד את כול חוקיו אשר צוה
לעשות ועל⌈ ⌉⌈פי ר<ו>ב⌉ ישראל המתנדבים
לשוב ביחד לבריתו

2 לעשות על פי רוב ישראל המתנדבים
לשוב ביחד ולהכתב איש לפני רעה
בסרך איש לפי שכלו

23 וכתבם בסרכ איש לפני רעהו לפי שכלו

3 ומעשיו בתורה להשמע הכול איש לרעה[ו] הקטן
לגדול ולהיות

ומעשיו להשמע הכול איש לרעהו הקטן
לגדול ולהיות

4QSᵈ] ואשר לוא יוכל 1QS [ואשר לוא יאכל ואל, based on some traces in 4QSᵇ. ‖ ⌈ואש⌉ר לוא ⌈יתבור⌉ עמו בהון וב⌈עודה⌉ other hand, proposes מאומה of 1QS, the scribe apparently first wrote a *vav* as the second letter, then corrected it to an *aleph*. At the end of the word, the scribe also seems to have first written an *aleph*, then corrected it to a *he*. ‖ **16–18** כול מידם יקח ולוא ישתה ולוא כול מהונם מאומה אשר לוא במחיר כאשר כתוב חדלו לכם מן האדם אשר נשמה באפו כיא במה נחשב הואה כיא כול אשר לוא נחשבו בבריתו להבדיל 1QS] אותם ואת⌈כול⌉ 4QSᵈ. At this point, the text in 4QSᵈ differs greatly. There is no equivalent in 1QS for the partially preserved phrase of 4QSᵈ lines 9–10 ○[ ]ל[איש מאנשי הקדש] . **18** Word space in ואת⌈כול⌉ not extant in 1QS. ‖ 4QSᵈ ולא ישענו 1QS] ולוא ישען. In 4QSᵈ, the verb ישענו may alternatively be read as ישנעו, containing a scribal transposition. ‖ איש הקודש 1QS] > 4QSᵈ ‖ וכול מעשיהם 1QS] ומעשיהם 4QSᵈ ‖ להשמיד 1QS] ישמיד 4QSᵈ ‖ ההבל 1QS] הבל 1° 4QSᵈ ‖ **19** הבל 1QS] הקודש 1QS > 4QSᵈ ‖ In the copy text of 4QSᵈ, some letters in לנד⌈ה⌉ לפ[נ]⌈ו⌉ are supplied by 4QSᵇ. ‖ **20** In 4QSᵈ, some commentators restore the end of line 11 of that manuscript on the basis of 1QS 5:20: [הונם בכ]⌈ל⌉ וטמא. It is unclear, however, whether any of the text after לנד⌈ה⌉ לפ[נ]⌈ו⌉ (the word is partially preserved in 4QSᵇ as well) actually followed 1QS, for soon after, the preserved text is quite different from that in 1QS. ‖ **20–21** וכיא יבוא בברית לעשות ככול החוקים האלה ליחד לעדת קודש ודרשו את⌈ ⌉⌈רוחום ביחד בין איש לרעהו לפי שכלו 1QS > 4QSᵈ. Some remains of text have been preserved, but they do not seem to correspond to that in 1QS. Compare especially the words]ם גוים ושבעות וחרמים ונדרים בפיהם [ ] in line 12 of 4QSᵈ. ‖ **21** Word space in את⌈ ⌉⌈רוחום not extant in 1QS. ‖ ומעשיו 1QS] ואת מעשיהם 4QSᵈ ‖ ביחד 1QS > 4QSᵈ ‖ **22** ⌈חוקיו⌉ 1QS] ח⌈ו⌉ק[י]⌈ו⌉ 4QSᵍ ‖ ⌈פי⌉ 1QS] ועל⌈ ⌉⌈פי 4QSᵈ. Word space in ועל⌈ ⌉⌈פי not extant in 1QS. ‖ ולהכתב 1QS] וכתבם 4QSᵈ ‖ **23** 4QSᵈ,ᵍ > 1QS] לבריתו 4QSᵍ ‖ לשבת יחד 4QSᵈ, 1QS] לשוב ביחד in 1QS. ‖ את מעשיהם 4QSᵈ. In 1QS [?]⌈ו⌉לרעה[ו] איש 4QSᵍ] לרעהו איש 4QSᵈ ולכת⌈ב⌉ איש לפנ[י] רע[ה] בסרך איש לפ[י שכל]ו 4QSᵈ; it is unclear whether the *lacuna* included the suffix similarly to רעהו of lines 4, 5, and 6 of column II of that manuscript or whether the text here had only רעה, as in 4QSᵈ II, 2. ‖ ומעשיו בתורה 1QS] ומעשיו 4QSᵈ, [ה]⌈בתור⌉ ומעשו 4QSᵍ ‖

17 *except for payment, as it is written, "Have no more to do with man in whose nostrils is breath, for what is he worth?" For*

18 *all those who are not counted in his covenant, they and everything that belongs to them are to be kept separate.* No *man of holiness* shall rely on any deeds

19 of vanity, for vanity are all those who do not know his covenant. He will destroy from the earth all those who spurn his word, and *all* their deeds are impure

20 before him, and all their wealth unclean. When a man enters into the covenant to act according to all these statutes that he may join the congregation of holiness, they shall examine

21 *his spirit in common, distinguishing between one man and another, with respect to his insight* and *his* deeds in regard to the law, under the authority of the sons of Aaron who have willingly offered themselves *in the community* to establish

22 his covenant and to pay attention to all his statutes that he has commanded men to perform, *and* under the authority of the multitude of Israel who have willingly offered themselves to return in the community *to his covenant.*

23 *They shall register them in the order, one before another* according to his insight and his deeds, that they may all obey one another, the one of lower rank obeying the one of higher rank. They shall

10 [   ] l [   ] No *one* shall rely on an[y de]eds

of vanity, for vanity are all those who do not [know his covenant.] He will destroy from the earth [all those who spur]n his word, and their deeds are impure] bef[or]e him [ ] l [ ]

12 [   ]m gentiles. Oaths, dedications, and vows are in their mouths [   ]

13]dšl[   ]l[   ]

4QSᵈ II

1a and *their* deeds in regard to the law, under the authority of the sons of Aaron who have willingly offered themselves to establish

1b his covenant and to pay attention to all his statutes that he has commanded men

2 to perform under the authority of the multitude of Israel who have willingly offered themselves to return in the community.

They shall be registered, one before another, in the order, each man according to his insight

3 and his deeds *in the law*, that they may all obey one another, the one of lower rank obeying the one of higher rank. They shall

	4QSᵈ II		1QS
4a	פוֹקְדִים את רוחם ומעשיהם	24	פוקדם את⌐ ⌐רוחם ומעשיהם שנה בשנה
	בתורה שנה בשנה ל⌐ה⌐עלות איש כפי		להעלות איש לֹפי שכלו ותום דרכו ולאחרו
	שכֹ[לו] ולאחרו כנעותיוֹ להוכיח		כנעויתוֹ להוכיֹ⌐ח⌐
4b	איש את רעהו ואהבת חסד	25	איש את רעהו בא[מ]ֹת וענוה ואהבת חסד
			⌐לאיש vacat אל ידבר ⌐אליהו⌐ באף או
			בתלונה
5a	ואל ידבר איש אל רעהו באף או	26	או בעורף [קשה] ⌐או בקנאת⌐ רוח רשע ואל
	בתלונה א⌐ו⌐ בקנאת רשע		ישנאהו [ ] [לֹ] לבבו כיא ביומ<> יוכיחנו
			ולוא

	4QSᵈ II (cont.)		Column VI (1QS)
5b	וגם אל יבא איש על רעהו דבר לרבים	1	ישא עליו עוון וגם אל יביא איש על רעהו דבר לפני
			הרבים אשר לוא בתוכחת לפני עדים ב>ᵃ<לה
6	אשר לא בהוכֹח לפני עֹ⌐ד⌐ים ⌐וֹבאלה יתהלבֹו בכל	2	יתהלכו בכל מגוריהם כול הנמצא איש את רעהו
	מגוריהם כל הנמצא את רעהו ויֹשֹ[מ]ֹ⌐ע הקטן⌐		וישמעו הקטן לגדול למלאכה ולממון ויחד יואכלו
7	לגדול למלאכה ולֹ°[ ]כלו יֹ[ח]ֹדֹ יברֹכו ויחד	3	ויחד יברכו ויחד יועצו ובכול מקום אשר יהיה שם
	יועֹצֹו ו[ב]ֹכול מֹ[ ]קום אשר יֹהֹיֹה שם⌐ [עשרה]		עשרה אנשים מעצת ⌐היחד⌐ אל ימש מאתם איש

1QS 6:1–27 — 4QSⁱ 1–5 (par. 1QS 6:1–4); 4QSᵈ II, 5–10 (par. 1QS 6:1–7); 4QSᵍ 2 1–5 (par. 1QS 6:3–5); 4QSᵈ III, 1–3 (par. 1QS 6:9–12); 4QSᵇ XI, 5–8 (par. 1QS 6:10–13); 4QSᵇ XI, 11–13 (par. 1QS 6:16–18); 4QSᵍ 3 1–4 (par. 1QS 6:22–25); 4QSᵍ 4 1 (1QS 6:27)

5:24 פוקדם 1QS] פוקדים 4QSᵈ ‖ Word space in ⌐את⌐ ⌐רוחם⌐ not extant in 1QS. ‖ ומעשיהם בתורה 1QS] ומעשיהם 4QSᵈ, ⌐ומעשי⌐הם 4QSᵍ ‖ להוכיֹח of 1QS, the scribe has redrawn כנעויתוֹ 4QSᵈ ‖ כנעויתוֹ 1QS] כנעותיוֹ 4QSᵈ ‖ ותום דרכו 1QS > 4QSᵈ ‖ כפי 1QS] לפי 4QSᵈ, בֹ[תורה] 4QSᵍ ‖ In להוכיֹ⌐ח⌐ of 1QS, the scribe has redrawn כ and written a ḥet above the line. ‖ **25** איש 1QS > 4QSᵈ ‖ לאיש 1QS > 4QSᵈ ‖ בא[מ]ֹת וענוה 1QS > 4QSᵈ ‖ איש את רעהו 4QSᵈ. In אליהוה 1QS] אליהו 4QSᵈ ‖ אליהוה of 1QS it is likely that the scribe erroneously repeated the singular suffix הו-. The word is to be read אליהו, as suggested by Lohse 1986, 20. In 4QSᵈ the scribe has explicated the implied referent (רעה) that in 1QS is expressed by a suffix. ‖ **26** או בעורף [קשה] 1QS > 4QSᵈ ‖ For [קשה] בעורף, see 1QS 4:11. In 4QSᵈ או בקנאת is preserved, so the text in 1QS can be reconstructed on the basis of that manuscript. ‖ ואל ישנאהו [ ] [לֹ] לבבו כיא ביומ<> יוכיחנו 5:26–6:1 ‖ בקנאת רשע 4QSᵈ] בקנאת רוח רשע 1QS ‖ בתוכחת 1QS] דבר לרבים 1QS] דבר לפני הרבים 1QS > 4QSᵈ ‖ **6:1** יבא 4QSᵈ,ⁱ (orth./gram.?) ‖ יביא 1QS] יבא 4QSᵈ ‖ ולוא ישא עליו עוון 1QS > 4QSᵈ ‖ וֹבאלה 1QS] בֹ>ᵃ<לה 1QS ‖ וֹבאלה 4QSᵈ ‖ In the copy text of 4QSᵈ, some letters in ⌐וֹ⌐באלה and עֹ⌐ד⌐ים are supplied by 4QSⁱ. ‖ בהוכֹח 4QSᵈ ‖ **2** את רעהו 4QSᵈ ‖ איש את רעהו 1QS ‖ In the copy text of 4QSᵈ, some letters in ⌐ויֹשֹ[מ]ֹע הקטן⌐ have been supplied by 4QSⁱ. ‖ וישמעֹ 4QSⁱ. It is likely, but not certain, that the reading in 4QSᵈ agrees with the one in 4QSⁱ: וישמעו הקטן לגדול 1QS ‖ ולהֹ[ן] 4QSᵈ, ולממון 1QS, ולהון 4QSⁱ (err.) ‖ למלאכה 1QS, למלאכה⌐ 4QSᵈ, וישֹ⌐מע הקטן⌐ 4QSᵈ. In 4QSᵈ line 7, it is unclear whether the word following למלאכה in 4QSᵈ is ולממון, as in 1QS, or ולהון, as in 4QSⁱ. ‖ **3** יחד 1QS] יֹ⌐ח⌐דֹ 4QSᵈ. In יחד 2°, the scribe first started the word with a lamed, probably followed by a he or a ḥet, then erased them and wrote וי instead. ‖ In 1QS, the word החיד has yod and ḥet transposed. Read היחד. ‖ In the copy text of 4QSᵈ, the words ⌐מֹ[ ]קום אשר יֹהֹיֹה שם⌐ have been supplied by 4QSⁱ. ‖ **3–4** מאתם איש כוהן 1QS] מ[אתם כו]ֹהן 4QSᵈ

24 review their spirits and their deeds every year that they may promote each man *according* to his insight *and the perfection of his way*, or demote him according to his perversity. They shall reprove

25 one another *in tr[uth], humility*, and kindly love *toward man*. Let no man speak to his neighbor in anger or in complaint

26 or *with a [stiff] neck [or in a jealou]s spirit of* wickedness, and *let him not hate him [...] of his heart. But let him reprove him on the same day lest*

review their spirits and their deeds

4a *in the law* every year that they may promote each man *in accordance with* his insight or demote him according to his perversity. They shall reprove

4b one another in kindly love.

5a *And* let no man speak to *another* in anger or in complaint or in jealous wickedness

Column VI (1QS)

1 *he incur guilt because of him*. And let no man bring a matter against his neighbor before the many except after reproof before witnesses. In these (ways)

2 shall they all walk in all their dwelling places, whenever *each man* encounters his neighbor. The one of lower rank shall obey the one of higher rank in regard to work and money. Together they shall eat,

3 together they shall pray, and together they shall take counsel. In every place where there are ten men from the council of the community, let there not be lacking among them *a man*

4QSᵈ II (cont.)

5b and let no man bring a matter against his neighbor before the many

6 except after reproof before witn[esses]. *And* in these (ways) shall they walk in all their dwelling places, whenever *one* encounters his neighbor. [The one of lower rank shall] obey the one of higher rank in regard to work and [money.   ...]*klu*, toge[ther] they

7 shall pray, and together they shall take coun[sel.] In e[very pl]ace where there are [ten]

4	כוהן ואיש כתכונו ישבו לפניו וכן ישאלו לעצתם לכול דבר והיה כיא יערוכו השולחן לאכול או ⸢התירוש⸣		8	אנשים מ֯[עצת היחד אל ימש מ]א֯תם כו֯[הן וא]י֯[ש כתכונו יש]ב֯ו
5	לשתות הכוהן ישלח ידו לרשונה להברך בראשית הלחם⸢		9	והיה כי [יערוכו השולחן לאכול או הת]י֯רוש֯] לשתות ה[כ]והן יש֯לח
6	והתירוש ואל ימש במקום אשר יהיו שם העשרה איש דורש בתורה יומם ולילה		10	והתירוש] [קד] [
7	תמיד ⸢חליפות⸣ איש לרעהו והרבים ישקודו ביחד את שלישית כול לילות השנה לקרוא בספר ולדרוש משפט			
8	ולברך ביחד vacat הזה הסרך למושב הרבים איש בתכונו הכוהנים ישבו לרשונה והזקנים בשנית ושאר			

4QS^d II

9	כול העם ישבו איש בתכונו וכן ישאלו למשפט ולכול עצה ודבר אשר יהיה לרבים להשיב איש את מדעו		1	איש את מד[עו
10	לעצת היחד vacat אל ידבר איש בתוכ֯ דברי רעהו טרם יכלה אחיהו לדבר vacat וגמ֯ אל ידבר לפני תכונו הכתוב			[י֯דבר֯]
11	לפניו האיש הנשאל ידבר בתרו ובמושב הרבים אל ידבר איש כול דבר אשר לוא להפצ הרבים וכיא האיש		2	הרבים אל ידב[ר
12	המבקר על הרבים וכול איש אשר יש אתו דבר לדבר לרבים אשר לוא במעמד האיש השואל את עצת		3	לרבים אשר]

6:4 כתכונו 1QS, 4QS^d, 4QS^g] בת[כונו 4QSⁱ ‖ In והיה, the scribe may have first written *aleph* as the last letter of the word, then corrected it to *heh*. ‖ Word space in ⸢או התירוש⸣ not extant in 1QS. ‖ **4–6** The text of 1QS includes a dittography: the words או התירוש לשתות הכוהן ישלח ידו לרשונה להברך בראשית הלחם have been repeated. In line 5, the ceiling brackets indicate the position of the deletion. ‖ **7** In 4QS^d line 10, if the word of which two letters are preserved is קד]יש, corresponding to ישקוד of 1QS 6:7, the text in 4QS^d was shorter than in 1QS. ‖ 1QS reads על יפות, but most scholars propose a textual emendation here: חליפות. ‖ **8** The ink in the right leg of the first *he* in הזה has rubbed off, but it is unlikely that there would have been a deliberate erasure here. **9–13** The text in 4QS^d, preserved only very fragmentarily, was shorter than in 1QS. It appears that וגמ אל ידבר לפני תכונו הכתוב in 1QS 6:10–11 was an intentional addition. The proposals for reconstructing the text in 4QS^d vary; compare, e.g., Metso 1997, 43; and Alexander and Vermes 1998, 103. A partial parallel to the text of 1QS 6:10–13 is also preserved in 4QS^b XI, 5–8. Alexander and Vermes (1998, 55) propose that]י֯דבר[of 4QS^b XI, 5 overlaps with the latter part of the line in 1QS 6:10: וגמ אל ידבר לפני תכונו הכתוב. In light of 4QS^d, however, it is more likely that]י֯דבר[of 4QS^b XI, 5 corresponds to an earlier phrase אל ידבר איש בתוכ in the same line and that the clause starting with וגמ was missing altogether. ‖ **10** In the second *vacat*, there are traces of smudged ink.

4 *who* is a priest; they shall sit before him, each according to his rank, and in the same order they shall be asked their counsel in regard to any matter. When they prepare the table to eat or the new wine

5 to drink, the priest shall first stretch out his hand to bless the firstfruits of the bread …

6 … and the new wine. In the place where there are ten men, let there not be lacking a man who studies the law day and night

7 continually, one man being replaced by another. And the many shall watch together for a third of all the nights of the year to read the book, to study the law,

8 and to pray together. This is the rule for a session of the many. Each (shall sit) according to his rank. The priests shall sit in the first seats, the elders in the second, and then the rest

9 of all the people shall sit, each according to his rank. In the same order they shall be asked for judgment or concerning any counsel or matter that has to do with the many, each man offering his knowledge

10 to the council of the community. No man shall interrupt his neighbor's words before his brother has finished speaking or speak before one registered in rank

11 before him. A man who is asked shall speak in his turn. In the session of the many, no man shall say anything that is not approved by the many and, indeed, by the overseer

12 of the many. Any man who has something to say to the many but is not entitled to question the council

8 men from [the council of the community, let there not be lacking among] them a priest; they shall si[t   ]

9 When [they prepare the table to eat or the n]ew win[e to drink, the] priest shall stret[ch out   ]

10 and the new wine[   ]*qd*[   ]

4QS^d II

1 each man [offering] his knowledge [   ]

]shall interrupt[

2 of the many no man shall sa[y   ] […]

3 to the many but is [   ]

6:4-6 1QS contains a dittography: the words "or the new wine to drink, the priest shall first stretch out his hand to bless the first fruits of the bread" have been accidentally repeated. They have been deleted in the translation. ‖ **7** The text parallel to 1QS 6:6b–7a was apparently shorter in 4QS^d, but the text is too fragmentary there to be fully reconstructed. ‖ **9–13** The text of 1QS is here about twice as long as in 4QS^d, but due to the fragmentary state of 4QS^d, it is difficult to get a clear idea how exactly the text differed. Presumably at least the words after the *vacat* of line 10 in 1QS, starting with וגם ('or…'), were missing in 4QS^d, since וגם is a commonly used redactional technique for additions.

4	ה[י]חד	13 היחד ועמד האיש על רגליהו ואמר יש אתי
		דבר לדבר לרבים אם י̇א̇ ו̇מרו לו

4QSb XI

8	]י̇ד̇ב̇ר̇ וכול ה̇מת[נדב	ידבר וכולה מת̇נדב מישראל 14 להוסיף על עצת היחד ידורשהו האיש הפקיד ברואש
		הרבים לשכלו ולמעשיו ואם ישיג מוסר מוסר יביאהו
		15 בברית לשוב לאמת ולסור מכול עול ז<ה>בינהו
		בכול משפטי היחד ואחר בבואו לעמוד לפני הרבים
		ונשאלו
11	]הכול[	16 הכול על דבריו וכאשר יצא הגורל על עצת הרבים
		יקרב או̇ י̇רחק ובקורבו לעצת היחד לוא יגע
		בטהרת
12	ב[ט̇הרת הרבים עד] מ̇[ו̇]לאת	17 הרבים עד אשר ידרושהו לרוחו ומעשו עד מלאת לו
		שנה תמימה וגם הואה אל יתערב בהון הרבים
13	[לו̇] שנה תמימה ישא[לו	18 ובמולאת לו שנה בתוך היחד ישאלו הרבים על
		דבריו לפי שכלו ומעשיו בתורה ואם יצא לו הגורל
		19 לקרוב לסוד היחד על פ̇י̇ הכוהנים ורוב אנשי בריתם יקר<י>בו גם את הונו ואת מלאכתו אל יד האיש
		20 המבקר על מלאכת הרבים יכתבו בחשבון בידו ועל הרבים לוא יוציאנו במשקה הרבים עד
		21 מולאת לו שנה שנית בתוך אנשי היחד ובמולאת לו השנה השנית יפקודהו על פי הרבים ואם יצא לו
		22 הגורל לקרבו ליחד יכתבהו בסרך תכונו בתוך אחיו לתורה ולמשפט ולטוהרה ולערב את הונו ויה̇יה̇ עצתו
		23 ליחד ומשפטו *vacat*

ל

	vacat 24	ואלה̇ המשפטים אשר ישפטו בם במדרש יחד על פי הדברים אם ימצא בם איש אשר ישקר
		25 בהון והואה יודע ויבדילהו מתוך טהרת רבים שנה אחת ונענשו את רביעית לחמו *vacat* ואשר ישיב את

6:13 Note that the copy text at this point changes to 4QSb, starting with 4QSb XI, 8. ‖ יומרו 1QS. ‖ י̇א̇ ו̇מרו] 1QS [וכולה מת̇נדב
וכול ה̇מת[נדב 4QSd. This variant may have been created by a simple scribal error, and the *he* at the end of וכולה most likely should
be read adjoined with the next word, i.e., המת̇נדב. ‖ **15** The scribe first wrote ולבינהו, then erased the first *vav* and the upper
stroke of *lamed*, turning the *lamed* into a *vav*. He added a superlinear *he*, thus resulting in והבינהו. ‖ **15–17** The text in 4QSb was
shorter than in 1QS. On the basis of the spacing of the preserved parts, it is possible that phrases וכאשר יצא הגורל על עצת הרבים
יקרב או̇ י̇רחק (1QS 6:16) and וגם הואה אל יתערב בהון הרבים (1QS 6:17) were missing in 4QSb, but since so little is preserved and
there are variants in the extant words in 6:17, no reconstruction is offered. ‖ **17** The words עד אשר ידרושהו לרוחו ומעשו seem not
to have been included in 4QSb, since the letter following עד plus a *lacuna* of one letter cannot have been a *shin* of אשר, for the
stroke is too deep. Rather, it was more likely the bottom stroke of the *mem* in מ̇[ו̇]לאת; see Tucker 2019, 185–92. This variant
gives an indication that a shorter version of the text in 4QSb may have extended at least to the end of column VI in 1QS. Too
little of the text in 4QSb is preserved, however, to present the parallel texts side by side from 1QS 6:19 onward. ‖ **18** בתוך היחד
1QS] תמימה 4QSb. ‖ **19** In 1QS, there is no word space extant in על̇ פ̇י̇. ‖ **20** In the second word of the line in 1QS, the scribe
first wrote אל, then corrected it into על by reshaping the first letter. ‖ **24** בם במדרש יחד 1QS] > 4QSg ‖ **25** בהון 1QS [במ[מון 4QSg
וה[בדילהו 1QS] ויבדילהו 4QSg ‖ והואה 1QS] והוא 4QSg.

COLUMN VI

13 of the community shall stand on his feet and say, "I have something to say to the many." If they tell him to speak,

    4 the [comm]unity

4QS[b] XI

he shall speak. Anyone who willingly offers himself from Israel

    8 he shall speak. Anyone who willin[gly offers himself

14 to join the council of the community, the officer in charge at the head of the many shall examine him with respect to his insight and his deeds. If he is suited to the discipline, he shall admit him

15 into the covenant that he may return to the truth and turn aside from all injustice and shall instruct him in all the rules of the community. And afterwards, when he comes to stand before the many, they shall all be asked

16 about his affairs, *and as the decision is taken on the advice of the many*, he shall either draw near or keep away. If he draws near to the council of the community, he shall not touch the purity

    11]all[

17 of the many until *they have examined him with respect to his spirit and his deeds while* he completes a full year, *nor shall he have any share in the wealth of the many.*

    12]the purity of the many while he[ ]completes

18 When he has completed a year *in the midst of the community*, the many shall be asked about his affairs with respect to his insight and his deeds in regard to the law. If, on the advice of the priests and the multitude of the men of their covenant, the decision is taken for him

    13]a full year [the many] shall be ask[ed

19 to draw near to the fellowship of the community, both his wealth and his property shall be handed to the overseer

20 of the property of the many; he shall enter it in the account with his own hand but shall not spend it on the many. He shall not touch the drink of the many until

21 he has completed a second year in the midst of the men of the community. When he has completed a second year, he shall be examined on the authority of the many. If the decision is taken for him

22 to draw near to the community, they shall register him in the order of his rank among his brothers, with respect to law, judgment, purity, and for pooling his wealth. His counsel

23 and his judgment shall be available to the community.

ך

24 These are the rules by which they shall judge at a community inquiry according to the cases. If a man is found among them who has knowingly lied

25 about wealth, they shall exclude him from the purity of the many for one year, and he shall be fined a quarter of his food. Whoever answers

26 רעהו בקשי עורף ⸢ידבר בקוצר אפים לפׄרוע את יסוד עמיתו ב⸢ה ⸢מרות את פי רעהו הכתוב לפניהו

27 [ה]ׄוׄשיעה ידו ⸢לוׄ ⸢ונ<אׄ>עׄנׄ⸢ש שנה אח]ת ומובדל וא[שׄר יזכיר דבר בשם הנכבד על⸢ ⸢כול הׄ○] [

Column VII (1QS)

1 ואם קלל או להבעת מצרה או לכול דבר אשר לו <׃ ׃ ׃ ׃ ׃> הואה קור⸢אׄ⸢ בספר או מברך והבדילהו

2 ולוא ישוב עוד על עצת היחד vacat ואם באחד מׄן הכוהנים הכתובים בספר דבר בחמה ונענש שנה

3 אחת ומובדל על נפשו מן טהרת רבים ואם בשגגה דבר ונענש ששה חודשים vacat ואשר יכח⸢שׄ⸢ במדעו

4 ונענש ששה חודשים והאיש אשר יצחה בל⸢י משפט את רעהו בדעהא ונענש שנה אחת

5 ומובדל ואשר ידבר את רעהו במרום או יעשה רמיה במדעו ונענש ששה חודשים ואם

6 vacat ברעהו ⸢יתרמה ונענש שלושה חודשים vacat ואם בהון היחד יתרמה לאבדו ⸢ישלמו < >

7 ברושו vacat

vacat

8 ואם לוא תשיג ידו לשלמו ונענש ששים ⸢יום ואשר יטו⸢ר לרעהו אשר לוא <>בׄמשפט ונענש (ששה חודשים) שנה אחת

9 וכן לנוקם לנפשו כול דבר ואשר ידבר בפיהו דבר נבל שלושה חודשים ולמדבר בתוך דברי רעהו

10 עשרת ימים ואשר ישכוב וישן במושב הרבים שלושים ימים וכן לאיש הנפ<>טׄר במושב הרבים

11 אשר לוא בעצה והנם עד שלוש פעמים על מושב אחד ונענש עשרת ימים ואם יזׄ<>קׄפוׄ

12 ונפטר ונענש שלושים יום ואשר יהלך לפני רעהו ערום ולוא היה אנוש ונענש ששה חודשים

1QS 7:1–25 — 4QS^g 4 2–6 (par. 1QS 7:1–4); 4QS^e I, 4–15 (par. 1QS 7:8–15); 4QS^g 5 1–9 (par. 1QS 7:9–14); 4QS^d V, 1 (par. 1QS 7:13); 4QS^g 6 1–5 (par. 1QS 7:15–18); 4QS^e II, 3–8 (par. 1QS 7:20–25); 11Q29 (par. 1QS 7:18–19)

6:26 For באמרות in 1QS, read בהמרות. ‖ **27** In 1QS, instead of לוא, read לו. ‖ In the word ונ<אׄ>עׄנׄש in 1QS, the scribe—immediately after writing an *aleph*—seems to have wiped it off, for the surface of the letter is not scratched. He made a second error later in the word, however, by transposing the order of the second *nun* and *ayin*. Read ונענש. ‖ The reconstruction of the second *lacuna*, אח]ת ומובדל וא[שׄר, is based on 1QS 7:3, 5. ‖ In 1QS, the word space is not extant in ⸢כול על⸢. ‖ **7:1** The erasure in 1QS after לו was made using both a sharp instrument and cancellation dots. ‖ In 1QS, read קורא as קורה (orth./phon.?). ‖ **2** In the context, מׄן seems to be the most likely reading, but the shape of the *mem* is very unusual, more similar to a *bet*. ‖ **3** In 1QS, the scribe first wrote אל, then corrected it to על. ‖ 4QS^g לרבים [1QS רבים. ‖ The reading in 1QS is יכחש. Although Clines (1993–2014) lists כחס as the root here, this is the only known occurrence of that root. It is more likely that the scribe made a sibilant error for כחש. ‖ **6** In 1QS columns VII–VIII, there are a number of *vacats* in unexpected places, such as here at the beginning of line 6. It is possible that the *Vorlage* that the scribe was using was so poorly preserved that he could not read it properly and therefore left empty spaces for later emendation. ‖ **8** In משפטׄ of 1QS, the scribe appears to have written המשפט first. ‖ In 1QS, there appear to be parentheses surrounding ששה חודשים. The parentheses are faded enough to suggest they were erased. Compare the erased letters before משפט. In any case, an alternative punishment of שנה אחת is written above the line. In 4QS^e I, 4 three letters are preserved:]שׄים[. They should presumably be taken as corresponding to the text of 1QS: ששה חודשים. No parenthesis appears after [שׄים] in 4QS^e. ‖ **10** 4QS^e,i ישכב [1QS ישכוב. ‖ 4QS^e ממוש הרבים, 4QS^g 1QS, במושב הרבים. ‖ **11** In וחׄנם of 1QS, *het* seems to have been written over *ayin*. ‖ **12** Instead of אנוש in 1QS, in 4QS^g Alexander and Vermes (1998, 181) read אנוס, but the reading is questionable. B-365864 (plate 705 frag. 10) shows a split down the center of the character, and the piece on the left is placed too close to the one on the right. The remaining ink strokes are compatible with other *shin*s in the fragment, whereas no *samek* to compare is preserved anywhere in 4QS^g.

26 his neighbor with obstinacy or speaks to him impatiently, ig[nor]ing the dignity of his companion by rebelling against the command of his neighbor who is registered before him,

27 [has] taken the law into his own hands. He shall be fined for on[e] year [and excluded. Who]ever affirms anything by the name of the one honored above all [...]

Column VII (1QS)

1 If he has blasphemed, either through being terrified by distress or whatever reason he may have, while he is reading the book or praying, they shall exclude him,

2 and he shall never return to the council of the community. If he has spoken in anger against one of the priests registered in the book, he shall be fined for one year

3 and excluded on his own from the purity of the many. But if he spoke through inadvertence, he shall be fined for six months. Whoever lies knowingly

4 shall be fined for six months. The man who knowingly and without cause insults his neighbor shall be fined for one year

5 and excluded. Whoever speaks deceitfully to his neighbor or knowingly acts deceitfully shall be fined for six months. If

6 he is negligent toward his neighbor, he shall be fined for three months. But if he is negligent with regard to the wealth of the community so that he causes its loss, he shall restore it

7 in full.

8 If he is unable to restore it, he shall be fined for sixty days. Whoever bears a grudge against his neighbor without cause shall be fined for six months/one year.

9 And likewise for anyone who avenges anything himself. Whoever speaks with his mouth anything foolish: three months. For the one who interrupts his neighbor's words:

10 ten days. Whoever lies down and falls asleep during a session of the many: thirty days. And likewise for the man who leaves a session of the many

11 without permission and without reason as many as three times in one session—he shall be fined for ten days, but if he leaves while they are standing,

12 he shall be fined for thirty days. Whoever goes naked before his neighbor without being compelled to do so shall be fined for six months.

13 ואיש אשר ירוק אל תוך מושב הרבים ונענש שלושים יום vacat ואשר יוציא ידו מתוחת בגדו והואה
14 פוח ונראתה ערותו ונענש שלושים יום ואשר ישחק בסכלות להשמיע קולו ונענש שלושים
15 יום והמוציא אתˀ ידˀ שמאולו לשוח בה ונענש עשרת ימים והאיש אשר ילך רכיל ברעהו
16 והבדילהו שנה אחת מטהרת הרבים ונענש ואיש ברבים ילך רכיל לשלח הואה מאתם
17 ולוא ישוב עוד והאיש אשר ילון על יסוד היחד ישלחהו ולוא ישוב ואם על רעהו ילון
18 אשר לוא במשפט ונענש ששה חודשים והאיש אשר תזוע רוחו מיסוד היחד לבגוד באמת
19 וללכת בשרירות לבו אם ישוב ונענש שתי שנים ברשונה <׃> לוא יגע בטהרת הרבים
20 vacat < ׃ ׃ ׃ > ובשנית לוא יגע <׃ ׃ ׃> <משקה> הרבים ואחר כול אנשי היחד ישב ובמלואת
21 לו שנתים ימים ישאלו הרבים vacat על דבריו ואם יקרבהו ונכתב בתכונו ואחר ישאל ˀעˀל המשפט
22 < > <וכול איש אשר יהיה בעצת היחד> < > על מלואת עשר שנים
23 vacat < > vacat < > ושבה רוחו לבגוד ביחד ויצאˀ מˀלפני
24 הרבים ללכת בשרירות לבו לוא ישוב אל עצת היחד ואיש מאנשי היחˀד אˀשˀר יתערב
25 עמו בטהרתו או בהונו אשˀר [הרבים והיה משפטו כמוהו לשל]חו [

Column VIII (1QS)

1 בעצת היחד שנים עשר איש וכוהנים שלושה תמימׂים בכול הנגלה מכול
2 התורה לעשות אמת וצדקה ומשפט ואהבת חסד והצנע לכת איש ˀעˀם רעהו
3 לשמור אמונה בארץׁ ביצר סמוך ורוח נשברה ולרצת עוון בעושי משפט
4 וצרת מצרףׂ ולהתהלךׁ עםׂ כול ב<ˀעˀ>מדת האמת ובתכון העת בהיות אלה בישראל

1QS 8:1–27 — 4QS^e II, 9–18 (par. 1QS 8:1–10); 4QS^d VI, 1–12 (par. 1QS 8:6–21); 4QS^e III, 1–6 (par. 1QS 8:11–15); 4QS^d VII, 1–2 (par. 1QS 8:24–27)

7:13 The reading corresponding to 1QS ואשר יום שלושים is highly uncertain in 4QS^e. In particular, the ink marks in 4QS^e I, 11 do not support the presence of יום following the final *mem* of שלושים. Whether the ink marks represent ואשר (omitting יום) is also uncertain. The ink traces and spacing suggest a different reading altogether, perhaps extending to all three words. || 1QS [ידו] אˀתˀ ידˀו] 4QS^e. In 4QS^d, ידו is preserved, but the preceding word is not, so it is unclear which reading 4QS^d supports. || The text in 4QS^e is fragmentary, but one would expect to see some remains of a *vav* at the end of בגד. None can be seen, which opens the possibility that 4QS^e presents a variant and did not include the suffix. || **14** The scribe first wrote ונרעתה, then corrected it to ונראתה. || **15** Word space in אתˀ ידˀ not extant in 1QS. || **16** 1QS [לשלח הואה מאתם] ושלחוהומאˀתםˀ 4QS^e || 1QS [שלושים] ששים 4QS^g; no word space in 4QS^g after שלחוהו[ו. || **17** 1QS [ישלחהו] לשלח 4QS^g || **18** 1QS [רוחו מיסוד היחד לבגוד] רוחו לבגוˀדˀ 11Q29 || **20** Qimron reads רבים for the first erased word in 1QS and בטהרת for the second (Qimron and Charlesworth 1994b, 32; Qimron 2010, 222 with note), but it is difficult to verify these readings from the photographs. Both readings are possible. || **21** In 1QS, the second to last word of the line is written אל but should be understood as על. || **22** 1QS [על מלואת] עד מלאות לו 4QS^e || **23** In 1QS, the scribe wrote ויצאם and after a narrow word space לפני, an error for ויצא מלפני. || **24** The reading היחˀד אˀשˀר is preserved in 4QS^e. || **8:1** 1QS [איש] אנשים 4QS^e || In 1QS, perhaps the scribe accidentally wrote the singular form תמים, then corrected it into a plural. This explains the final *mem* in the middle of תמימׂים. || **2** 4QS^e [צדקה] וצדקה 4QS^e || For אמ in 1QS, read עמ. || **3** 1QS סמוך [סמוךˀ ובענבה 4QS^e || **4** 1QS [ולהתהלך] התהלך 4QS^e. Alexander and Vermes (1998, 139) read וׂהׂתהלך in 4QS^e, but there is no *vav*; rather, the upper stroke of a *lamed* a line below extends high enough to create an impression of an additional letter.

13 A man who spits into a session of the many shall be fined for thirty days. Whoever brings his hand out from beneath his garment and
14 is so raggedly dressed that his nakedness is seen shall be fined for thirty days. Whoever guffaws foolishly shall be fined for thirty
15 days. He who brings his left hand out to gesticulate with it shall be fined for ten days. The man who goes about slandering his neighbour
16 shall be excluded from the purity of the many for one year and fined. But a man who goes about slandering the community shall be sent away from them
17 and shall never return. The man who makes complaints about the authority of the community shall be sent away and shall not return. But if it is against his neighbour that he makes complaints
18 without cause, he shall be fined for six months. The man whose spirit so deviates from the fundamental principles of the community that he betrays the truth
19 and walks in the stubbornness of his heart, if he returns, he shall be fined for two years. In the first year he shall not touch the purity of the many,
20 and in the second he shall not touch the drink of the many, and he shall sit behind all the men of the community. When he has completed
21 two years, the many shall be asked about his affairs. If they allow him to draw near, he shall be registered in his rank, and afterwards he may be asked about judgement.
22 But no man who has been in the council of the community for ten full years
23 and whose spirit turns back so that he betrays the community, and who leaves
24 the many to walk in the stubbornness of his heart, shall ever return to the council of the community. Anyone from the men of the commun[ity who has any]thing to do
25 with him in regard to his purity or his wealth whi[ch…] the many, his sentence shall be the same: he shall be sent [away].

Column VIII (1QS)

1 In the council of the community (there shall be) twelve men and three priests, perfect in all that has been revealed from the whole
2 law, that they may practice truth, righteousness, justice, kindly love, and circumspection one toward another;
3 that they may preserve faithfulness in the land by a constant mind and a broken spirit; that they may pay for iniquity by the practice of justice
4 and (the endurance of) the distress of affliction; and that they may walk with all men according to the standard of truth and the rule of the time. When these exist in Israel,

5 נכונה ⟨ה⟩עצת היחד באמת ⟨ל⟩ *vacat* למ⟨ט⟩עת עולם בית קודש לישראל וסוד קודש

6 קודשים לאהרון עדי אמת למשפט וב⟨י⟩⟨חירי⟩ רצון לכפר בעד הארץ ולהשב

4QSᵈ VI		Column VIII (cont.)	
] 1	ול[ה]שיב לרשעים	7	לרשעים גמולם *vacat* היאה חומת הבחן פנת יקר בל *vacat*
] 2	ממ[קומם	8	יזדעזעו ᵞˢᵒᵈᵒᵗʸʰᵒ ובל יחישו ממקומם *vacat*
] 3a	מעון קודש קודשים	9	לאהרון בדעת כולם לברית משפט ולקריב ריח
]	בישרא[ל		ניחוח ובית תמים ואמת בישראל
] 3b	להקים ברית לחקות עולם	10	⟨להקם ברית לחו⟨קו⟩ת עולם⟩ והיו לרצון לכפר בעד הארץ ולחרוץ משפט רשעה ⟨ואין עולה⟩ בהכין
] 4	בי[סוד		
	היחד שנתים ימים		אלה ביסוד היחד שנתים ימים בתמים דרך
] 5	אנש[י היח]ד	11	יבדלו קודש בתוך עצת אנשי היחד וכול דבר
	נ[ס]תר מיש[ראל ונמצא		⟨נ⟩סתר מישראל ונמצאו לאיש
] 6	לאיש [*vacat*	12	הדורש אל יסתרהו מאלה מיראת רוח נסוגה
	ובהיות אלה[בישראל]יבדלו מ[תוך		*vacat* ובהיות אלה ליחד בישראל
] 7a	אנשי [	13	בתכונים האלה יבדלו מתוך מושב א⟨נשי⟩ העול ללכת למדבר לפנות שם את דרך הואהא

---

6 וב⟨י⟩⟨חירי⟩ ‖ 8:5 למ⟨ט⟩עת עולם 1QS [למ[שפט עולם 4QSᵉ. In 1QS, the scribe first wrote בעת עולם, then corrected it to למ⟨ט⟩עת עולם. ‖ וב⟨י⟩חירי 1QS] ובחרי 4QSᵉ. Most editions of 4QSᵉ read בחירי, but a close inspection of B-295975 reveals that no *yod* is attested between *het* and *resh*. The reading in 4QSᵉ is thus ובחרי, which corresponds to the original reading in 1QS before a supralinear *yod* was added. ‖ ולהשב 1QS] ול[ה]שיב 4QSᵈ, ᵉ⁽?⁾ ‖ **7** היא 1QS] היאה 4QSᵉ. In 4QSᵉ, Alexander and Vermes (1998, 139) read היאה, but B-284709 shows that there is no *he* following the *aleph*. Thus, the shorter form of the pronoun is attested in 4QSᵉ. ‖ **8** Although the text in both 4QSᵈ and 4QSᵉ is preserved only fragmentarily, space considerations indicate that the word יסודותיהו added above the line in 1QS was included in the text of 4QSᵈ but not in 4QSᵉ. ‖ In 4QSᵉ, although the downstroke of the *nun* in מעון is very short, the letter cannot be a *zayin* (מעוז) as suggested by Alexander and Vermes (1998, 139), for the top of the letter lacks the shape of *zayin* characteristic of the hand in 4QSᵉ. ‖ **10** In 1QS, it is not entirely clear whether some of the ink marks are erasure dots or remains of the erased word(s). ‖ להקם 1QS] להקים 4QSᵈ ‖ ולחרוץ משפט רשעה בעת לכפר לרצון והיו 1QS > 4QSᵉ ‖ **11** לקדש 4QSᵉ ‖ נסתר 1QS <> נ[ס]תר 4QSᵈ. In נ⟨ס⟩תר, the scribe seems to have started the word with a *taw* but then erased it partially, thereby creating a *nun*. ‖ ונמצא 4QSᵈ] ונמצאו 1QS; ונמצא[א 4QSᵉ ‖ **12** Some of the letters in 4QSᵉ have been rewritten, and the text is difficult to decipher. For discussion, see Qimron and Charlesworth 1994a, 86–87; Metso, 1997, 53–54; Alexander and Vermes 1998, 145–46; and Qimron 2010, 225. ‖ **12–13** בתכונים האלה ליחד בישראל אלה 4QSᵈ. Based on the line length in 4QSᵈ, it is unlikely that the words ליחד and בתכונים האלה added above lines 12–13 in 1QS were included in 4QSᵈ. ‖ יבדלו 1QS] יבדלו בישראל אלה 4QSᵈ. ‖ **13** In 1QS, in the phrase יבדלו מתוך מושב א⟨נשי⟩ העול, the word מתוך has been rewritten, but it is difficult to know what the original word was. In 4QSᵉ, the word מתוך is omitted, but the reading is not ממ[ו]שב, as suggested by Alexander and Vermes (1998, 144), but rather מושב. The *vav* is almost wholly preserved in 4QSᵉ, and uninscribed leather on the left bottom of the letter precludes the possibility that it would have been a second *mem*. The first two letters of the word are visible on B-295966, and the last two letters of the word are visible on B-295967. In light of this, there is a distinct possibility that the reading in 4QSᵈ VI, 6 would have followed that in 4QSᵉ. In 4QSᵈ, only מ[יבדלו is preserved, but it is unclear whether it belongs to מתוך or מושב. אנשי 1QS] הנשי 4QSᵈ. There is ink in 4QSᵉ, but the word is highly uncertain, possibly אנשי, as suggested by Alexander and Vermes (1998, 144). Qimron proposes that the word is in cryptic script (Qimron and Charlesworth 1994a, 86). ‖ המ[ד]בֿ[רה 4QSᵉ] למדבר 1QS. The suggestion of a locative *he* at the end

5   the council of the community shall be established in truth as an eternal plant, a holy house for Israel and a most holy assembly

6   for Aaron, witnesses of truth for the judgment and chosen by the will (of God), that they may make expiation for the land and pay

	Column VIII (*cont.*)		4QS^d VI

7   the wicked their reward. It shall be the tested wall, the precious cornerstone, whose foundations shall neither

1   [… and] pay the wicked

8   shake nor stir from their place. (It shall be) a most holy dwelling

2   [から th]eir place. (It shall be) a most holy dwelling

9   for Aaron, with all knowledge of the covenant of justice, and shall offer a soothing odor; and (it shall be) a house of perfection and truth in Israel

3a [in Isr]ael

10 that they may establish the covenant according to the eternal statutes. *And they shall be accepted to make expiation for the land and to determine the judgment of wickedness, and there shall be no more injustice.* When these have been established in the fundamental principles of the community for two years in perfection of way,

3b that they may establish the covenant according to the eternal statutes.

4   [in]the fundamental principles of the community for two years

11 they shall be set apart as holy within the council of the men of the community. And nothing that was hidden from Israel but found by the man

5   [the men] of the commu[nity was h[idden from Is]rael but found

12 who studies shall he hide from these through fear of an apostate spirit. When these exist as a community in Israel

6   by the man [ ]
    When these exist [in Israel] they shall separate themselves fr[om]

13 *in accordance with these rules*, they shall separate themselves from the settlement of the men of injustice and shall go into the wilderness to prepare there *the way of him,*

7   the men of [

44 THE COMMUNITY RULE

7b	התור[ה אשר צוה בי]ד מושה לעש[ות	15	היאה מדרש התורה ⌈אשר⌉ צוה ביד מושה	
	כו[ל] [ ]		לעשות ככול הנגלה עת בעת	
8a	ע]ת	14	כאשר כתוב במדבר פנוֹ דרך •••• ישרו בערבה	
			מסלה לאלוהינו	
8b	אי[ש מאנשי ברית	16	וכאשר גלו הנביאים ברוח קודשו vacat וכול	
	ה[י]חד [		איש מאנשי היחד ברית	
9	[...]	17	היחד אשר יסור מכול המצוה דבר ביד רמה	
			אל יגע בטהרת אנשי הקודש	
10	[...]	18	ואל ידע בכול עצתם עד אשר יזכו vacat מעשיו	
			מכול עול להלכׄ בתמים דרך וקרבהו	
		19	בעצה על פי הרבים ואחר יכת<ׄב> בתכונו	
11	[הנוסף] [ליחד] [		וכמשפט הזה לכול הנוספׄ ליחד ⌐	
		20	ואלה המשפטים אשר ילכו בם vacat	
			אנשי התמים קודש איש את רעהו	
12	[ ] [כל ה]בא [ל]ׅ[ע]צת [	21	כול הבא בעצת הקודש ההולכים בתמים	
			דרכׄ כאשר צוה כול איש מהוׄה	
		22	אשר יעבר דבר מתורת מושה ביד רמה או	
			ברמיה ישלחהו מעצת היחד	
4QSᵈ VII		23	ולוא ישוב עוד ולוא יתערב איש מאנשי	
			הקודש בהונו ועם עצתו לכול	
1a	והבדילהו מן הטהרה ומן העצה ומן	24	דבר ואם בשגגה יעשה והובדל מן הטהרה	
	המשפט שנת[ים ימ]ים		ומן העצה ודרשו המשפט	
		25	אשר לוא ישפוט איש ולוא ישאל על כול	
			עצה שנתים ימים אמ⌈ ⌉תתם דרכו	
1b	ושב במדרש ובעצה אם לא הלך עוד	26	במושב במדרש ובעצה [ע]ׅ[פׅ]יׄ הׄרׄבׄיׄםׄ	
2a	בשגגה עד מלאות לו שנתים		אם לוא שגג עוד עד מולאת לו שנתים	
		27	ימים vacat	

---

of the word is by Alexander and Vermes (1998, 146). ‖ שם 1QS] שמ[ה̇ 4QSᵉ ‖ הואהא 1QS] האמת 4QSᵉ. In 1QS, the spelling הואהא with *aleph* at the end is unique. It occurs nowhere else in the nonscriptural or scriptural corpus of the Dead Sea Scrolls. ‖ **14** Although the text in 4QSᵈ is fragmentary, it is clear that the quote of Isa 40:3, added in 1QS 8:14, was not included in 4QSᵈ. ‖ **15** Both 1QS and 4QSᵉ seem to be reading the feminine form היאה here, *pace* Alexander and Vermes (1998, 144). ‖ אשר is fully preserved in 4QSᵈ. In 1QS, it is only partially preserved: א̇[ש]ׅרׅ. ‖ ביד מושה לעשות 1QS] ביד משה אלה החקים 4QSᵉ. In 4QSᵉ, a large passage comprising 1QS 8:15b–9:11 is missing. ‖ **16–17** מאנשי ברית היחד 1QS] מאנשי ברית 4QSᵈ ‖ כבול 1QS] כל 4QSᵈ ‖ **21** בעצת 1QS] לׅ[עצת 4QSᵈ ‖ **24** והובדל 1QS] והבדילהו 4QSᵈ ‖ ודרשו המשפט 1QS] ומן המשפט 4QSᵈ ‖ **25** אשר לוא ישפוט איש ולוא ישאל על כול עצה 4QSᵈ] 1QS ‖ ⌈תתם⌉ אמ⌈ ⌉ not extant in 1QS. ‖ **25–26** תתם דרכו במושב 4QSᵈ] תתם דרכו ושב 1QS ‖ Word space in 4QSᵈ **26** הׄרׄבׄיׄםׄ [פׅ]ׄיׄ [ע]ׄ 1QS] <עפי> 4QSᵈ ‖ אם לוא שגג עוד 1QS] אם לא הלך עוד בשגגה 4QSᵈ ‖ מולאת 1QS] מלאות 4QSᵈ ‖ ושב 1QS] 4QSᵈ ‖ **26–27** שנתים 1QS] שנתים ימים 4QSᵈ ‖

14 *as it is written: "In the wilderness prepare the way of* ....; *make level in the desert a highway for our God."*

15 This (way) is the study of the law t[hat] he commanded through Moses, that they should act in accordance with all that has been revealed from time to time

7b of the l]aw that he commanded thro[ugh Moses, that th]ey should act in acc[ordance]

8a time[

16 and in accordance with what the prophets revealed by his holy spirit. No man from among *the men of the community, the covenant*

8b No man from among *the men of the covenant of the com[munity*

17 *of the community*, who presumptuously leaves unfulfilled any one of the commands shall touch the purity of the men of holiness

9 [...]

18 or know any of their counsel until his deeds have been cleansed from all injustice by walking in perfection of way. Then they shall admit him

10 [...]

19 to the council on the authority of the many, and afterward he shall be registered in his rank. In accordance with this rule (they shall treat) all who join the community.

11 [join] the community

20 These are the rules by which the men of perfect holiness shall walk with one another.

21 Everyone who joins the council of holiness, (the council) of those who walk in perfection of way in accordance with what he has commanded—every man of them

12 [ ] Everyone who [join]s the c[ouncil]

22 who transgresses a word from the law of Moses presumptuously or negligently shall be sent away from the council of the community

23 and shall never return; no man from among the men of holiness shall have anything to do with his wealth or with his counsel in regard to any

4QS^d VII

24 matter. But if he acted through inadvertence, he shall be excluded from the purity and from the council, *and they shall consult the rule:*

1a he shall be excluded from the purity and from the council *and from the decision making* for tw[o yea]rs

25 *"He shall not judge anyone or be asked for any counsel for two years."* If his conduct is perfect

26 *in session*, in study, and in council [*according to the man*]*y*, if he does not *act inadvertently* again throughout two

1b *and shall return* in study and in council if he does not *act through inadvertence* again

27 years—

2a throughout two years

---

15 The section 1QS 8:15b–9:11 is lacking in 4QS^e.

COLUMN IX (1QS) — 4QS^d VII (cont.)

4QS^d VII (cont.)		1QS Column IX	
כי על שגגה אחת יענש שנתים וליד	2b	כיא על <> שגגה אחת יענש שנתים ולעושה ביד	1
הרמה לא ישוב עוד אך		רמה לוא ישוב עוד אך השוגג	
שנתים [י]מים יבחן לתמים דרכו ולעצתו על פי	3	יבחן שנתים ימים לתמים דרכו ועצתו על פי הרבים	2
הרבים ונכתב בתכונו ליחד קודש		ואחר יכתוב בתכונו ליחד קודש	
[בהיו]ת אלה בישראל ליחד כתכונים האלה ליֹסד	4	vacat בהיות אלה בישראל ככול התכונים האלה	3
רוח קודש לאמת עולם לכפר על אשמת פשע		ליסוד רוח קודש לאמת	
[ומעל חטא]ת ולרצון לאר[ץ מבשר] עלות וחלבי	5	עולם לכפר על אשמת פשע ומעל חטאת ולרצון	4
זבחים ותרומות ונדבת שפתים למ[שפ]ט כניחוח		לארץ מבשר עולות ומחלבי זבחֿ ֗ותרומת	
[צדק ותמים]דֿרך כנדב[ת מנחת ר]צֿון בעת	6	שפתים למשפט כניחוח צדק ותמים דרך כנדבת	5
ההיא יבדלו בית אהרון לקודש לכל ○[ ]○ל		מנחת רצון בעת ההיאה יבדילו אנשי	
		היחד בית קודש לאהרון להיֹחד קודש קודשים ובית	6
		יחד לישראל ההולכים בתמים	
[ ]לישׂ[ר]אל ההלכים בתמֹי[ם רק בני אה]רׂן	7	רק בני אהרון ימשלו במשפט ובהון ועל פיהם יצא	7
ימש[ל]וׂ ב[משפט וֹבהון vacat וֹהוׂן] [		הגורל לכול תכון אנשי היחד	
[ההולכי]ם בתמים אל יתע[רב הונם ע]ם[הון] אנשי	8a	והון אנשי הקודש ההולכים בתמים אל יתערב הונם	8
הר[מ]יֹה [אשר]		עם הון אנשי הרמיה אשר	
לא הזכ[ו] [	8b	לוא הזכו דרכם להבדל מעול וללכת בתמים דרכֿ	9
		ומכול עצת התורה לוא יצאו ללכת	
[ ]רׂ[ ] להתֿהֹלךׂ ב[ ] ונשפטו	9	בכול שרירות לבם ונשפטו במשפטים הרשונים אשר	10
בם]		החלו אנשי היחד לתיסר בם	

1QS 9:1–26 — 4QS^d VII, 2–9 (par. 1QS 9:1–10); 4QS^e III, 6–19 (par. 1QS 9:12–20); 4QS^d VII, 13–VIII, 1–10 (par. 1QS 9:15–26); 4QS^b XVIII, 1–7 (par. 1QS 9:18–23); 4QS^e IV, 1–6 (par. 1QS 9:20–24); 4QS^f I, 1–2 (par. 1QS 9:23–24)

9:1 ולעושה ביד רׄמה 1QS] ולידׄ הרמה 4QS^d ‖ השוגג 1QS] > 4QS^d ‖ **2** יבחן שנתים ימים 1QS] [מים יבחן [י]שנתים 4QS^d ‖ ועצתו 1QS] ולעצתו 4QS^d ‖ ואחר יכתוב 1QS] ונכתב 4QS^d **3** ככול התכונים 1QS] כתכונים ליחד 4QS^d ‖ **4–5** ותרומת֗ ֗זבחֿ ומחלבי 1QS] תרומת שפתים 4QS^d ‖ **5–6** וחלבי זבחים ותרומות ונדבת שפתים 4QS^d. In 1QS, the word space is not extant in ותרומת֗ זבחֿ. **5** יבדילו 1QS] יבדלו 4QS^d ‖ ועל פיהם יצא והגורל 7 1QS] בית אהרון לקודש לכל ○[ ]○ל 4QS^d ‖ אנשי היחד בית קודש לאהרון להיֹחד קודש קודשים ובית יחד 1QS] > 4QS^d ‖ **8** The word הקודש was written over other letters in 1QS. Three letters in the middle of the word were erased, and an erasure dot was placed above before correcting to read הקודש. **9** וללכת 1QS] להתֿהֹלךׂ 4QS^d ‖ **9–10** Based upon the preserved ink marks in line 9 of 4QS^d, it is unclear to what extent its text corresponded to that of 1QS. The text in 1QS appears to have been longer. For discussion, see Alexander and Vermes 1998, 111 and 114.

COLUMN IX (1QS)

1. because it is for one sin of inadvertence that he is punished for two years, whereas the one who acts presumptuously shall never return. Only *the one who sins inadvertently*
2. shall be tested for two years with regard to the perfection of his way, and his counsel on the authority of the many, and *afterward* he shall be registered in his rank in the community of holiness.
3. When these exist in Israel in accordance with *all* these rules as a foundation of the spirit of holiness in eternal truth,
4. to make expiation for the guilt of transgression and the unfaithfulness of sin, and that the land may be accepted without (or: through) the flesh of burnt offerings and without (or: through) the fat of *sacrifice*—and the proper offering
5. of the lips is like a soothing (odor) of righteousness and perfection of way like an acceptable freewill offering—at that time *the men of the community* shall separate themselves
6. as a holy house for Aaron, that they may be united as a holy of holies and as a house of community for Israel, for those who walk in perfection.
7. Only the sons of Aaron shall rule in matters of justice and wealth, *and on their word the decision shall be taken with regard to every rule of the men of the community.*
8. And the wealth of the men of holiness who walk in perfection, their wealth shall not be mixed with the wealth of the men of deceit who
9. have not made their way clean by separating themselves from injustice and by walking in perfection of way. They shall not depart from any counsel of the law to walk
10. in all the stubbornness of their heart, but they shall be governed by the first rules in which the men of the community began to be instructed

4QS^d VII (cont.)

2b. because it is for one sin of inadvertence that he is punished for two years, whereas the one who acts presumptuously shall never return. But
3. he shall be tested for two years with regard to the perfection of his way, and his counsel on the authority of the many, and he shall be registered in this rank in the community of holiness.
4. [When these ex]ist in Israel *for the community* in accordance with these rules as a foundation of the spirit of holiness in eternal truth to make expiation for the guilt of transgression
5. [and the unfaithfulness of s]in, and that the land may be accepted [without (or: through) the flesh of] burnt offerings and the fat of *sacrifices and offerings, and the proper freewill offering* of the lips is like a soothing (odor) of
6. [righteousness and perfection] of way like an acceptable freew[ill offering]—at that time *they* shall separate themselves as a holy house for Aaron *to all* [...]
7. fo]r Israel, for those who walk in perfection. Only the sons of Aaron shall rule in matters of justice and wealth. And the wealth [...]
8a. who walk in perfection, their wealth shall not be mixed with the wealth of the men of deceit who
8b. have not made cle[an   ]
9.] *shall walk with* [   ], but they shall be governed by the [   ]

---

4 The translation of the Hebrew preposition in "without (or: through)" is ambiguous. Either meaning is possible. ‖ **10** The text parallel to 1QS 9:9–10 was different and shorter in 4QS^d, but the text in 4QS^d is only fragmentarily preserved.

48 THE COMMUNITY RULE

11 עד בוא נ͏ביא ומשיחי אהרון וישראל vacat

12 vacat אלה החוקים למשכיל להתהלך בם עם כול חי לתכון עת ועת ולמשקל איש ואיש

13 לעשות את רצון אל ככול הנגלה לעת בעת וללמוד את כול השכל הנמצא לפי העתים ואת

14 חוק העת להבדיל ולשקול vacat בני הצדוק לפי רוחום ובבחירי העת להחזיק על פי

13 ואיש [כבר כ]פיו לקרבו

4QS^d VIII

15 רצונו כאשר צוה ואיש כרוחו כן לעשות משפטו ואיש כבור כפיו לקרבו ולפי שכלו

1 ולפי שכלו להגישו וכן אהבתו עם שנאתו ואשר

16 להגישו וכן אהבתו עם שנאתו vacat ואשר לוא להוכיח ולהתרובב עם אנשי השחת

לא יוכיח איש ולא יתרובב עם אנשי ה^שח<ע>ת

17 ולסתר את עצת התורה בתוך אנשי העול ולהוכיח דעת אמת ומשפט צדק לבוחרי

2 ולסתר עצתו בתוך אנשי העול ולהוכיח דעת אמת ומשפט צדק לבחירי דרך איש כרוחו וכתכון

18 דרך איש כרוחו כתכון העת ולהנחותם בדעה וכן להשכילם ברזי פלא ואמת בתוך

3 העת ל͏הנחות͏ם בדעה וכן להשכילם ברזי פלא ואמת בתוך אנשי היחד להלך תמים איש את

19 אנשי היחד לה<>לך תמים איש את רעהו בכול הנגלה להם <ה͏>היאה עת פנות הדרך

4 ר͏עהו בכול [ה]נגלה להם היא עת פנות הדרך למדבר להשכילם בכל הנמצא לעשות בעת

20 למדבר ולהשכילם כול הנמצא לעשות בעת הזואת והבדל מכול איש ולוא הסר דרכו

5 [הזואת והבדל] מכל איש אשר לא הסיר דרכיו מכול עול vacat ואלה תכוני הדרך למשכיל בעת[ים]

21 מכול עול vacat ואלה תכוני הדרך למשכיל בעתים האלה לאהבתו עם שנאתו שנאת עולם

9:11–12 The space between lines 11 and 12 is unusually large, equal to an uninscribed line in between. ‖ **13** In 4QS^e III, 8, it is difficult to determine the word preceding רצון. The reading in 1QS is לעשות את רצון, but Alexander and Vermes (1998, 144, 146) suggest לע͏שות רצון in 4QS^e. ‖ לפי] 1QS ‖ לפ͏ני] 4QS^e ‖ **14** את בני הצדק] 1QS ‖ בני הצדק] 4QS^e ‖ רוחום] 1QS ‖ ר[ו]ח͏מה] 4QS^e ‖ **15** לא יוכיח איש ולא יתרובב] 1QS ‖ לוא להוכיח ולהתרובב] 4QS^d ‖ In 4QS^d, the word ה^שח<ע>ת has an erasure dot above the *ayin*. ‖ **16** [פ]ל] 4QS^e ‖ לופי] 1QS, 4QS^d ‖ עצתו] 4QS^d ‖ את עצת התורה] 1QS, 4QS^e ‖ ולסתיר] 4QS^e ‖ ולסתר] 1QS, 4QS^d ‖ **17** לבחירי] 1QS ‖ לבוחרי] 4QS^d, (?) ‖ להנ͏] 1QS ‖ וכתכונו] 4QS^e ‖ וכתכונ͏י] 4QS^d; וכתכון] 1QS כתכון] 4QS^e II, 15. See also 1QS 8:6 and par. ‖ **18** ולהנחותם] 1QS, 4QS^d ‖ ו͏להנחות͏ם of 1QS, *taw* is redrawn. The reading is not entirely certain. ‖ **18–19** ואמת בתוך אנשי [ה]נחות͏ם] 4QS^d ‖ In חותם 4QS^b, ‖ ה͏יחד 1QS, 4QS^d ‖ ו͏אם תיתם דרך סוד ה͏י͏חד] 4QS^e **19** רעהו] 1QS, 4QS^b] רע͏רו] 4QS^e. The reading in 4QS^e contains a scribal error and should be corrected to רעהו. Alexander and Vermes (1998, 145) follow Qimron and Charlesworth (1994a, 88) in reading רעיו, but the top left stroke of the third letter is broad and does not correspond to the sharp hook of a *yod* typical of the hand in 4QS^e. ‖ איש ולוא] 1QS 4QS^b, d, e ‖ בכל] 1QS כול] 4QS^e ‖ ולהמשיל] 4QS^e ‖ ולהמשילם] 4QS^b, d ‖ להשכילם] 1QS ‖ ולהשכילם **20** היא] 4QS^e היאה] 1QS, <ה͏>היאה ‖ **20** איש אשר לא הסיר דרכיו] 4QS^d. The reading in 4QS^b is only partially preserved, but the last word of the phrase, דר[כו], in 4QS^b agrees with the form in 1QS; see Qimron 1986, §200.18 and 322.141. ‖ **21** In למשכיל in 1QS, the scribe appears first to have made a spelling error; the letter preceding the second *lamed* has been redrawn, and the *lamed* seems to have been slightly raised because of the minimal space.

11 until the coming of the prophet and the messiahs of Aaron and Israel.

12 These are the statutes by which the wise leader shall walk with every living being according to the rule appropriate to each time and according to the weight of each man.

13 He shall do the will of God in accordance with all that has been revealed from time to time. He shall learn all the wisdom that has been found throughout time and the

14 statute of time. He shall separate and weigh the sons of righteousness according to their spirit. He shall keep firm hold of the chosen ones of the time in accordance with

15 his will, in accordance with what he has commanded. He shall administer justice to each man according to his spirit. He shall admit each man according to the cleanness of his hands and cause him to approach according to his insight.

16 And likewise his love and his hatred. He shall not argue or quarrel with the men of the pit

17 but shall hide *the counsel of the law* in the midst of the men of injustice. He shall admonish with true knowledge and righteous judgment those who choose

18 the way, each man according to his spirit and according to the rule of the time. He shall guide them with knowledge and likewise instruct them in the mysteries of wonder and truth in the midst

19 of the men of the community that they may walk perfectly with one another in all that has been revealed to them. This is the time to prepare the way

20 to the wilderness, and he shall teach them everything that has been found to be done at this time and to separate themselves from every man who has not turned his *way*

21 from all injustice. These are the rules of conduct for the wise leader in these times with regard to his love and his hatred. (He shall maintain) eternal hatred

13 admit each man]according to the cleanness of his h[ands

4QS^d VIII

1 and cause him to approach according to his insight. And likewise his love and his hatred. He shall not argue or quarrel with the men of the pit

2 but shall hide *his* counsel in the midst of the men of injustice. He shall admonish with true knowledge and righteous judgment those who choose the way, each man according to his spirit and according to the rule

3 of the time. He s[hall guide] them with knowledge and likewise instruct them in the mysteries of wonder and truth in the midst of the men of the community that they may walk perfectly with one

4 [another in all that has been re]vealed to them. This is the time to prepare the way to the wilderness, and he shall teach them *in* everything that has been found to be done at

5 [this time and to separate themselves] from every man who has not turned his ways from all injustice. These are the rules of conduct for the wise leader in these times

50 THE COMMUNITY RULE

6	[האלה לאהבתו עם [שנאתו שנאת עולם עם אנשי
	השחת ברוח הסתר ולעזוב למו הון ובצע
7	[ועמל כפים כעבד למוש[ל בו וענוה לפני הרודה בו
	ולהיות איש מקנא לחוק ועתו ליוֹם נָקָֹם ל[עשות]
8	[רצון בכול משלח כפים וב[כֹ]וֹל ממשלו כאש[ר צוה
	וכו[ל הנעשה בו ירצֹה בנדבה וזולת רצון [אל לא
9	[יחפץ ובכול אמרי פיהו ירצה ולוא יתאוה ב[כֹוֹ]ל
	אשר לא צוה ולמש[פט אל יצפה ת[מיד]
10	[ ] ובכול אשר יהיה יֹס[פֹר
	[ ] תרומת שפתים י[ברכנו עם [קצים אשר

22	עם אנשי שחת ברוח הסתר לעזוב למו הון ועמל
	כפים כעבד למושל בו וענוה לפני
23	הרודה בו ולהיות איש מקנא לחוק ועתו ליום נקם
	לעשות רצון בכול משלח כפים
24	ובכול ממשלו כאשר צוה וכול הנעשה בו ירצה
	בנדבה וזולת רצון אל ל[וא] יחפץ
25	[ו]בֹכֹוֹל אמרי פיהו ירצה ולוא יתאוה בכול אשר לוא
	צוֹה לֹמֹשפט אל יצפה תמיד
26	[ ]קֹה יברכ עושיו ובכול אשר יהיה יסֹפֹ]ר
	תרומת שפתים יברכנו

4QS^d VIII (cont.)   COLUMN X (1QS)

11	[חקק אל בראשית ממשלת אור ע[ֹם ת]קופתו
	ובהא[ספו אל מעון חק]וֹ [בראשיֹת [אשמורי]
12	[חושך כיא יפתח אוצרו וישתהו עלת [ו]בתקופתו עם
	האספו מפ[ני אור בהופעֹ] מאורות מזבול קודשו
13	]עם האספם למעון כבוד במבוא מועדי ל[ֹם ליֹמי
	חודש יחד תקופתם עם מסרו[ת]ֹם זה לזה

1	vacat עם קצים אשר]חקק אל] ברשית ממשלת
	אור עמֹ תקופתו ובהאספו על מעון חוקו ברשית
2	אשמורי חושך כיא יפתח אוצרו וישתהו]על תבל
	ובתקופתו עם האספו מפני אור באופיע
3	מאורות מזבול קודש עם האספם למעון כבוד במבוא
	מועדים לימי חודש יחד תקופתם עם

4QS^d IX

1	בהתחדשם יום גדול לקודש קודשים ואות למפתחֹ
	חסדו עולם

4	מסרותם זה לזה בהתחדשם יום גדול לקודש קודשים
	ואות נ vacat למפתח חסדיו עולם לראשי

1QS 10:1–26 — 4QS^d VIII, 10–13 (par. 1QS 10: 1–3); 4QS^f II, 1–5 (par. 1QS:10:1–5); 4QS^b XIX, 1–6 (par. 1QS:10:3–7); 4QS^d IX, 1–12 (par. 1QS 10:4–12); 4QS^f III, 1–3 (par. 1QS 10:9–11); 4QS^d X, 1–8 (par. 1QS 10:12–18); 4QS^b XX, 1–7 (par. 1QS 10:13–18); 4QS^f IV, 1–10 (par. 1QS 10:15–20); 4QS^f V, 1–7 (par. 1QS 10:20–24)

9:22 שחת 1QS] השחת 4QS^d (orth./gram.?) משלוח 1QS] משלח 4QS^f ‖ **23** הון ובצע 4QS^d] הון 1QS ‖ ולעזוב 4QS^d] לעזוב 1QS, 4QS^e ‖ **24** The reading in 1QS is לו, but in the context it should clearly be understood as a negative לוא. ‖ **25** For אל, the name of God, 4QS^d uses Paleo-Hebrew. ‖ After the parallel of 1QS 9:25, 4QS^e starts with the text of 4QOtot (4Q319), in place of the hymn paralleling 1QS 9:26–10:22. ‖ **26** The reconstruction of תרומת [שפתים is based on 1QS 10:6 par. 4QS^b XIX, 4. ‖ **10:1** It is not entirely clear whether the scribe intentionally added a *vacat* after עם or whether there already was a defect or a hole (visible now) in the leather that the scribe had to get around. ‖ [חקק אל] חקק 1QS. The reading in 1QS, חקקא, is either a scribal error or a deliberate abbreviation. ‖ [על תבל] 4QS^f א[ש]מֹורות 4QS^f] אשמורי 1QS ‖ **10:2** בראשית 4QS^d, f] 1QS 2° ברשית 4QS^d] אל 1QS ‖ עלת 1QS. In 1QS, the reading עלת is possibly a deliberate abbreviation, or the *Vorlage* was too damaged to read properly. The word space following *taw* is slightly larger than normal; cf. the *nun* in 1QS 10:4. ‖ ובתקופתו 1QS] בתקופתו 4QS^f ‖ באופיע 1QS] בהופע 4QS^d ‖ קודש 1QS 3 קודשו 4QS^b] במבוא 1QS] וֹבֹבֹוֹא 4QS^f ‖ In 4QS^b, לימי has been written above the line. ‖ תקופתם 1QS, 4QS^d] תקופתיהֹמֹה 4QS^b. Alexander and Vermes (1998, 59) read תקופֹתֹיֹהֹמֹה in 4QS^b XIX, 2, but there is no *vav* between *pe* and *taw* in the manuscript. ‖ **4** נ 1QS] > 4QS^b, d. The solitary medial *nun* following ואות was written by the scribe of 1QS by mistake or perhaps because of an unreadable *Vorlage*. ‖ חסדי 1QS] חסדו 4QS^d; see Qimron 1986, §200.18 and 322.141.

COLUMN X

22 toward the men of the pit in a spirit of secrecy. He shall leave to them wealth and *wages* like a slave to his master and an oppressed man before

23 the one who rules over him. He shall be a man zealous for the statute and its time, until the day of vengeance. He shall do the will (of God) in everything he undertakes

24 and in everything he controls, as he has commanded. He shall willingly delight in everything that happens to him and have no pleasure in anything except the will of God.

25 [In al]l the words of his mouth he shall delight and shall not desire anything that he has not commanded but shall watch continually for the decision of God.

In 4QS[e], Otot (4Q319) starts here.

26 [...] he shall bless his maker, and in everything that happens he shall rec[ount... With the offering] of the lips he shall bless God

COLUMN X (1QS)

1 at the times he has ordained: at the beginning of the dominion of light, when it rises, and when it is gathered in to its appointed abode;

2 at the beginning of the watches of darkness, when he opens its storehouse and lets it out into the world, and when it sets and is gathered in prior to the light; at the emergence of

3 the luminaries from *the holy realm* and at their being gathered to the abode of glory. At the introduction of the seasons at the (first) days of the month as well as at their turning points

4 and when they succeed each other. Their renewal is a great day for the holy of holies and a sign of the opening of his everlasting *mercies*

---

6 [with regard to his love and] his hatred. (He shall maintain) eternal hatred toward the men of the pit in a spirit of secrecy. He shall leave to them wealth *and profit*

7 [and wages like a slave to his master and an oppressed man before the one who rules over him. He shall be a man zealous for the statute and its time, until the day of vengeance. He [shall do]

8 [the will (of God) in everything he undertakes and in every]thing he controls, as he has comma[nded]. He shall willingly delight in everything that happens to him and have [no pleasure] in anything except the will [of God].

9 [In all the words of his mouth he shall delight and shall not desire a]nything[that he has not commanded, but sha]ll watch continually [for the deci-]sion of God.

In 4QS[e], Otot (4Q319) starts here.

10 [... he shall bless his maker, and in everything that happens he shall rec]ount. With the offering] of the lips he shall bless him [at the times]

4QS[d] VIII (*cont.*)

11 [God has ordained: at the beginning of the dominion of light, w]hen it rises, and when it is gat[hered] in to its appointed abode; at the beginning [of the watches of]

12 [darkness, when he opens its storehouse and lets it out into the world, and when it sets and is gathered in pr]ior to the light; the luminaries from *his holy realm*

13 and at their being gathered to the abode of glory. At the introduction of the seasons at the (first) days of the month as well as at their turning points and when and when they suc[ce]ed each other

4QS[d] IX

1 Their renewal is a great day for the holy of holies and a sign of the opening of his everlasting *mercy*

5	מועדים בכול קץ נהיה vacat ברשית ירחים	2	לראשי מועדים בכל קץ נהיה ברואשית ירחים
	למועדיהם ימי קודש בתכונם לזכרון במועדיהם		למועדיהם ימי
6	< > תרומת שפתים ⸢אֲ⸣ברכנו כחוק חרות לעד	3	קודש בתכונם לזכרון במועדי⸢י⸣הם תרומת ⸢שֹׁפָּתֹ⸣י⸢ם⸣
	בראשי < > שנים ובתקופת מועדיהם בהשלם חוק		אברכנו כחק
		4	⸢ח⸣ו̇⸢ר⸣ות לעד בראשי שנים ובתקו[פ]⸢ו⸣ת מועדיהם
			בהש⸢ל⸣ם חוק
7	תכונם יום משפטו זה לזה מועד קציר לקיץ vacat	5	תכונם יום משפטו זה לזה מוע[ד] קציר לקיץ ומועד
	ומועד זרע למועד דשא מועדי שנים לשבועיהם		ז̇רע למועד
8	וברוש שבועיהם למועד דרור ובכול היותי חוק	6	דשא מועדי ש[ני]ם לשביעיה[ם וברוש ש[בֹעיהֹם
	חרות בלשוני לפרי תהלה ומנת שפתי <אשא>		למועדי דרור
		7	ובכל היותי חוק ח]רות ב̇[לשוני]תהלה ומ[נת]
			שפֹתי אזֹמרה̇
9	< > אזמרה בדעת וכול נגינתי לכבוד אל וכנור נבלי	8	בדעת וכל נגינתי לכבוד אל̇ [אֹכה נבל]י̇ לתכון]
	לתכון קודשו וחליל שפתי אשא בקו משפטו		קודשו וחליל]
10	עם מבוא יום ולילה אבואה בברית אל ועם מוצא	9	[שפתי א]שֹא בקֹו מ[שפטו עם מבוא] יום
	ערב ובוקר אמר חוקיו ובהיותם אשים		ו[לי]לֹ[ה] אבואה בברית
		10	[אל ועם מוצא ערב ובוקר אמר חוקיו]ובהיותם
			אשיב
11	גבולי לבלתי שוב ומשפטו אוכיח כנעויתי ופשעי לנגד	11	[גבולי לבלתי שוב ומשפטו אוכיח כנעויתי ופ]שעי
	עיני כחוק חרות ולאל אומר צדקי		לנגד עיני
		12	[כחוק חרות ולאל אומר צדקי ולעליון [מֹכֹין טֹו̇בֹי]
			מק]ו̇ר
12	ולעליון מכין טובי מקור דעת ומעין קודש רום כבוד	13	[דעת ומעין קודש רום כבוד
	וגבורת כול לתפארת עולם ⸢א⸣בחרה באשר		וגבורת כול לתפארת עולם אבחרה]

10:5 There is a *paragraphos* below line 5 in 1QS, although the ink is mainly lost. ‖ ברואשית 4QS^d, ברֹ^אשית 4QS^b, [ברשית 1QS ‖ **6** There are traces of ink at the beginning of the line, but it is not clear whether they are the result of an intentional erasure or are accidental smudges. ‖ אברכנו 4QS^b, d. The reading in 1QS is in error. ‖ **8** למועדי 4QS^d [למועד 1QS ‖ **9** In 4QS^d IX, 8, the name of God is written in Paleo-Hebrew. ‖ [אֹכה נבל]י̇] 4QS^d. Alexander and Vermes (1998, 161) suggest that 4QS^f read אֹכה נבלי with 4QS^d, but an inspection of an enlarged B-284303 shows that the first two letters in 4QS^f preserved are וכ. Both the spacing and the ink traces support the reading of 1QS וכנור נבלי. ‖ **10** In אבואה of 1QS, the fourth letter has been redrawn. The scribe appears to have first accidentally omitted the *aleph* and written *he* but, noticing his mistake, correctly spelled -אה. ‖ אשיב 4QS^d [אשים 1QS ‖ **12** The scribe in 1QS wrote erroneously הבחרה; read אבחרה. See a similar guttural error in 1QS 10:6.

COLUMN X

5   at the beginning of feasts in all times to come. At
6   the beginning of months at the times determined for them and on holy days according to their order, as a remembrance in their appointed times

6   I will bless him with the offering of the lips according to the statute engraved forever; at the beginning of years and at their appointed ends, when the statute of their rule is fulfilled

7   on the days appointed by him, which follow one another; from the time of the (early) harvest until the summer, from the time of sowing until the time of the emerging crop, on yearly feasts, which follow the weeks (of years),

8   from the beginning of their weeks (of years) to the *time* of jubilee. As long as I live, the engraved statute will be on my tongue as a fruit of praise and an offering of my lips.

9   I will sing with understanding, and all my music will be for the glory of God. *My lyre and* my harp accord with his holy order, and I will raise the flute of my lips according to his just measure.

10   At the arrival of day and night I will walk in the covenant of God; at the departure of evening and morning I will recite his statutes. When these occur I will set my

11   boundary so as not to turn back. I acknowledge his judgment concerning my sin. My iniquity is in front of my eyes like an engraved statute. I will say to God: "My righteousness,"

12   and to the Most High: "The one who prepares my good lot," "Well of Knowledge" and "Spring of Holiness," "Height of Glory" and "Omnipotent Eternal Splendor." I will choose what

---

2   at the beginning of feasts in all times to come. At the beginning of months at the times determined for them

3   and on holy days according to their order, as a remembrance in their appointed times I will bless him with the offering of the lips

4   according to the statute engraved forever; at the beginning of years and at their ap[po]inted ends, when the statute of their rule is fulfilled

5   on the days appointed by him, which follow one another; from the ti[me of the (early) harvest until the summer, from the time of sowi]ng until the time

6   of the emerging crop, on ye[ar]ly feasts, which follow their weeks (of years), [from the beginning of the w]eeks (of years) to the *times* of jubilee.

7   As long as I live, the [en]graved statute will be on [my tongue] as a fruit of praise and an off]ering of my lips. I will sing

8   with understanding, and all my music will be for the glory of God. *I will strike up* [my] harp in accord with his [holy] order, and I will raise [the flute]

9   [of my lips] according to his [j]ust meas[ure]. [At the arrival of] day and nig[ht] I will walk in the covenant of

10   [God; at the departure of evening and morning I will recite his statutes.] When these occur I will set my

11   [boundary so as not to turn back. I acknowledge his judgment concerning my sin. My ini]quity is in front of my eyes

12   [like an engraved statute. I will say to God: "My righteousness," and to the Most High:] "The one who prepares my good lot," "Well of

13   [Knowledge" and "Spring of Holiness," "Height of Glory" and "Omnipotent Eternal Glory." I will choose what]

13 יורני וארצה כאשר ישופטני בראשית משלח ידי ורגלי אברך שמו בראשית צאת ובוא

14 לשבת וקום ועם משכב יצועי ארננה לו ואברכנו תרומת מוצא שפתי במערכת אנשים

15 ובטרם ארים ידי להדשן בעדני תנובת תבל ברשית פחד ואימה ובמכון צרה עם בוקה

16 אברכנו בהפלא מ⌈א⌉ודה ובגבורתו אשוחח ועל חסדיו אשען כול היום ואדעה כיא בידו משפט

17 כול חי ואמת כול מעשיו ובהפתח צרה אהללנו ובישועתו ארננה יחד לוא אשיב לאיש גמול

18 רע בטוב ארדף גבר כיא את אל משפט כול חי והואה ישלם לאיש גמולו לוא אקנא ברוח

19 רשעה ולהון חמס לוא תאוה נפשי וריב אנשˢחת לוא א<   > נקם ואפיא לוא ⁽תפוש עד יום⁾

20 אשיב מאנשי עולה ולוא ארצה עד הכין משפט לוא אטור באף לשבי פשע ולוא ארחם

21 על כול סוררי דרך לוא אנחם בנכאים עד⌈ ⌉תום דרכם ובליעל לוא אשמור בלבבי ולוא ישמע בפי

22 נבלות וכחש עוון ומרמות וכזבים לוא ימצאו בשפתי ופרי קודש בלשוני ושקוצים

23 לוא ימצא בה בהודות אפתח פי וצדקות אל תספר לשוני תמיד ומעל אנשים עד תום

24 פשעם רקים אשבית משפטי נדות ונפתלות מדעת לבי בעצת תושיה אס⌈פ⌉ר דעת

25 ובערמת דעת אשוך [בעד]ה גבול סמוך לשמור אמנים ומשפט עוז לצדקת אל א̇ח̇לקה

26 חוק בקו עתים ו⌈ד⌉[   ]צדק אהבת חסד לנוכנעים וחזוק ידים לנמהר̇[   ]

10:13–15 The text in both 4QS^b and 4QS^d is only fragmentarily preserved, but the size of the lacunae indicates that in 4QS^d the text was shorter than in 1QS. No reconstruction of the shorter version is attempted here. For discussion, see Metso 1997, 47; and Alexander and Vermes 1998, 125. ‖ **13** ברשית] 1QS 1º ברא̇שית 4QS^b. The third letter of בראשית of 1QS has been redrawn. The scribe may have initially skipped the *aleph* and started drawing *shin* but, realizing his error, redrew the letter; it is unclear, however, what the scribe intended. Most editions (e.g., Burrows 1951, pl. X; Qimron 2010, 228) mark the letter as erased, but the leather shows no marks of scraping or visible erasure dots. ‖ **14** In 1QS, in the second-to-last word of the line, במערכת, the scribe wrote *bet* over an initial *mem*. ‖ **15** ברשית] 1QS בר⌈א⌉שית 4QS^f ‖ In ובמכון of 1QS, there is extra ink connecting the *bet* with the following *mem*. It appears that the scribe started drawing *mem* directly after *vav*. ‖ בוקא] 1QS בוקה 4QS^f ‖ **16** 1QS, מודה 4QS^b] מאדה 4QS^f. Read as מאודה. ‖ ואדעה כיא בידו 1QS, 4QS^b] > 4QS^f ‖ **18** לטוב] 1QS בטוב 4QS^f ‖ והואה] 1QS הוא 4QS^f ‖ **19** In ולהון of 1QS, the second *vav* appears to be written twice. ‖ In אנשˢחת of 1QS, the superlinear *shin* is a result of the scribe's initial haplography following אנש. ‖ In 1QS, the scribe erased three words except for the first *aleph* and wrote ⁽תפוש עד יום⁾א above the erasure. Qimron suggests that the erased text was א<טור באף לשבי>, but he notes (Qimron and Charlesworth 1994b, 45 n. 45) that the erased letters should not be read, for "it is an error introduced when the scribe let his eye wander to the next line in which these three words appear." ‖ ואפיא] 1QS ואפי 4QS^f ‖ **20** באף 1QS] > 4QS^f ‖ Following לשבי פשע, the text in 4QS^f (only partially preserved) appears to have differed from that of 1QS, since there is no correspondence in 1QS to אנשי of 4QS^f IV, 10. After לשבי פשע, the text in 1QS continues ולוא ארחם. Both 1QS and 4QS^f have preserved the words that follow: על כול סוררי דרך. ‖ **21** בנכוחים 4QS^f] בנכאים 1QS ‖ The word space in עד⌈ ⌉תום is not extant in 1QS. ‖ The last three letters of ובליעל in 1QS have been written over an erasure. The dot underneath ב appears accidental. ‖ **22** There appears to be a defect in the leather in 1QS under עוון, and the last two letters are slightly smudged. The scribe may have first written עול, then erased the third letter and corrected the word to עוון. ‖ **23** In 4QS^f, the word space is missing between אל and תספר. ‖ **24** Regarding אס⌈פ⌉ר in 1QS, the scribe wrote אסת̇ר, with *tav* as the third letter; he then placed a cancellation dot under it and the correct *pe* above it. ‖ **25** Guilbert (1961, 74–75 n. 110) suggests to reconstruct the lacuna as [בעד]ה on the basis of Job 1:10, and it makes sense in the context. ‖ **25** The top traces of letters preserved in the last word of the line in 1QS allow א̇ח̇לקה. ‖ **26** At the end of the line Guilbert (1961, 74–75 n. 116) reconstructs לנמה]רי לב according to Isa 35:4. Lohse (1986, 38) reconstructs [לנמה]רי לב וללמד. Qimron (2010, 228), however, reconstructs [לנמה]ים להודיע.

13 he teaches me and rejoice in how he judges me. Before I stretch my hand or foot, I will bless his name. Before I go out or come in,

14 sit down or get up, or lie down on my bed, I will rejoice in him and bless him with an offering that rises from my lips from among the ranks of men,

15 and before I raise my hand to nourish myself with the delicious bounty of the earth. At the onset of fear or terror in a place of distress and desolation,

16 I will bless him for his great wonders. I will meditate on his strength and rely on his mercies all day. I know that the judgment of all the living is in his hand

17 and that all his deeds are truth. When distress is released, I will praise him and rejoice in his salvation as well. I will repay no one the reward of evil

18 but strive for good for everyone, for to God belongs the judgment of all the living, and it is he who will give each his reward. I will not be zealous

19 in the spirit of falsehood, nor will my soul covet ill-gotten riches. I will not engage with the men of the pit until the day of vengeance, yet my hatred

20 will not turn from the men of injustice, and I will not be satisfied until judgment has been meted out. I will not bear a grudge in anger toward those who turn from evil, but I will have no pity

21 on those who rebel against the way. I will not comfort the smitten until their way is perfect. Belial I will not keep in my heart,

22 and no folly will be heard in my mouth, and no sinful lies, deceit or falsehood will be found on my lips. The fruit of holiness will be on my tongue,

23 and no abomination will be found there. In thanksgiving I will open my mouth; my tongue will tell without ceasing God's righteous deeds and the evil of men until their transgression ends.

24 Vanities I will remove from my lips, impurity and cunning from the knowledge of my heart. With wise counsel I will impart knowledge,

25 and with prudent knowledge I will fence it in within a firm boundary to guard faithfulness and strong judgment in accordance with God's righteousness. I will share

26 the statute with the measurement of the times […] righteousness and lovingkindness toward the downtrodden, encouragement to the alar[med, …]

Column XI

1 לתועי רוח בינה ולהשכיל רוכנים בלקח ולהשיב ענוה לנגד רמי רוח וברוח נשברה לאנשי
2 מטה שולחי אצבע ומדברי און vacat ומקני הון כיא אני לאל משפטי ובידו תום דרכי עמֿ ישור לבבי
3 ובצדקותו ימח פשעי כיא ממקור דעתו פתח אורו ובנפלאותיו הביטה עיני ואורת לבבי ברז
4 נהיה והוֹיֿא עולם משען ימיני בסלע עוז דרך פעמי מפני כול לוא ⸢יזדעזע⸣ כיא אמת אל היאה
5 סלע פעמי וגבורתו משענת ימיני וממקור צדקתו משפטי אור בלבבי מרזי פלאו בהוֿיֿא עולם
6 הביטה עיני תושיה אשר נסתרה מאנוש דעה ומזמת ערמה מבני אדם מקור צדקה ומקוה
7 גבורה עם מעין כבוד מסוד בשר לאש<ר> בחר אל נתנמ לאוחזת עולם וינחי<>לֿ>ם בגורל
8 קדושים ועם בני שמים חבר סודם לעצת יחד וסוד מבנית קודש למטעת עולם עם כול
9 קץ נהיה ואני לאדם רשעה ולסוד בשר עול עוונותי פשעי חטאתי < ׃ > עם נעוֿיֿת לבבי
10 לסוד רמה והולכֿי vacat חושך כיא לאדם דרכו ואנוש לוא יכין צעדו כיא לאל המשפט ומידו
11 תוםֿ הדרך ובדעתו נהיה כול ודול הוֿיֿה במחשבתו יכינו ומבלעדיו לוא יעשה vacat ואני אם
12 אמוט חסדי אל ישועתי לעד ואם אכשול בעוון בשר משפטי בצדקת אל תעמוד לנצחים
13 ואם יפתח צרתי ומשחת יחלץ נפשי ויכן לדרך פעמי ברחמיו הגישני ובחסדיו יביא
14 משפטי בצדקת אמתו שפטני וברוב טובו יכפר בעד כול עוונותי ובצדקתו יטהרני מנדת
15 אנוש וחטאת בני אדם להודות לאל צדקו ולעליון תפארתו < ׃ > <ברוך אתה אלי הפותח לדעה

ל

16 לב עבדכה הכן בצדק כול מעשיו והקם לבן אמתכה כאשר רציתה לבחירי אדם להתיצב
17 לפניכה לעד כיא מבלעדיכה לוא תתם דרך ובלי רצונכה לוא יעשה כול אתה הוריתה
18 כול דעה וכול הנהיה ברצונכה היה ואין אחר זולתכה להשיב על עצתכה ולהשכיל
19 בכול מחשבת קודשכה ולהביט בעומק רזיכה ולהתבונן בכול נפלאותיכה עם כוח
20 גבורתכה ומי יכול להכיל את כבודכה ומה אף הואה בן הֿאדם במעשי פלאכה

1QS 11:1-22 — 4QS^d XII, 4 (par. 1QS 11:7-8); 4QS^j 1-10 (par. 1QS 11:14-22); 4QS^d XIII, 1-3 (par. 1QS 11:14-15); 4QS^b XXIII, 1-3 (1QS 11:22)

11:3 As is the case with many letters in final position, *zayin* in ברז is somewhat larger. ‖ **4** In 1QS, read יזד עזרע as יזדעזע. ‖ **9** In 1QS, there are cancellation dots above and below the erased space of three letters preceding עם. ‖ **10** The negative לוא in 1QS should be understood as covering the previous clause as well; it is possible that the negative was lost before לאדם as a result of haplography. ‖ **11** In 1QS, note the final *kaph* in medial position in וֿדֿול, possibly covering over an erased letter. ‖ **15** The ink of the first letter of לאל is smudged. It is possible that the scribe started writing ע, anticipating עליון, but then corrected the letter into ל. Alternatively, the smudging was simply accidental. ‖ The scribe has placed dots above and below the space after תפארתו. ‖ **16** עבדכה 1QS] עבדך 4QS^j ‖ **17** לפניכה 1QS] לפניך 4QS^j ‖ מבלעדיכה 1QS] מבלעדיך 4QS^j ‖ הוריתה 1QS] [ה]ורית 4QS^j ‖ **18** עצתכה 1QS] [עצ]תֿךֿ 4QS^j ‖ **19** נפלאותיכה 1QS] נפלאותיך 4QS^j ‖ In 1QS, a crease in the leather slightly separates the first letter from the rest in עצתכה. ‖ **20** גבורתכה 1QS] גבורתך 4QS^j ‖ פלאכה 1QS] פלאך 4QS^j

Column XI

1 understanding to the erring spirit to teach instruction to those who grumble so they can answer with humility to the haughty and with a broken spirit

2 to oppressors, who point with a finger, speak falsehood, and seek riches. But as for me, my judgment is with God. In his hand is the perfection of my way and the uprightness of my heart,

3 and in his righteousness he will wipe away my sins. For from the well of his knowledge he has let forth his light, my eyes have seen his wondrous deeds, and my heart has been illumined with the mystery to come.

4 The Eternal One, he is the support of my right hand, and the road beneath my feet is on a solid rock that does not tremble in the face of anything. For the truth of God

5 is the rock beneath my feet, and his might is the staff of my right hand. From the well of his righteousness is my justice; the light in my heart is from his wondrous mysteries. Upon him who is forever

6 my eyes have gazed, wisdom hidden from humankind, knowledge and wise prudence (hidden) from mortals, the well of righteousness

7 and the reservoir of strength, as well as the spring of glory (hidden) from the council of humans. To those chosen by God, he has given them as an eternal possession, and he has bestowed upon them

8 the lot of the holy ones. With the heavenly beings he has joined their assembly as a council of the community, an assembly of the building of holiness, as an eternal planting

9 for all ages to come. As for me, I belong to sinful humankind and to the assembly of evil flesh. My transgressions and iniquities, my sins and the degradations of my heart

10 belong to the assembly of worms and to those who walk in darkness. For one's way is not his own, and no one can determine his own steps. For to God belongs the judgment, and from his hand is

11 perfection of the way. By his knowledge all things happen, and all that exists he establishes by his plan, and without him nothing is done. As for me,

12 if I stumble, the mercy of God is my everlasting salvation. If I trip by the iniquity of flesh, my judgment is by God's righteousness that stands forever.

13 If my distress is released, he delivers my soul from the pit and establishes my step on the way. By his compassion he has brought me near, and by his mercies comes my

14 justification. In his righteous truth he has judged me, and in his great goodness he will atone for all my transgressions. In his righteousness he will cleanse me

15 from the impurity of humankind and from the sinfulness of mortals to give thanks to God for his righteousness and to the Most High for his glory. Blessed are you, my God, who opens to knowledge

16 the heart of your servant. Establish in righteousness all his deeds, and strengthen the child of your handmaid, as is your wish for those chosen from mortals, so that he will serve

17 before you forever. For without you there is no perfection of the way, and without your will nothing is done. You have taught

18 all wisdom, and all that happens is by your will. There is no one beside you to dispute your counsel or comprehend

19 anything of your holy plan or perceive the depth of your mysteries or fathom any of your wonders or your mighty

20 power. And who can contain your glory? Indeed, what is a human being in the midst of your wonders?

21 וילוד אשה מה > ׃ < ישב לפניכה והואה מעפר מגבלו ולחם מדורו רמה מדורו והואה מצוררק

22 חמר קורץ ולעפר תשוקתו מה ישיב חמר ויוצר יד ולעצת מה יבין

ך

11:21 In 1QS between מה and ישב, the scribe placed dots above and below the line to mark a word division that he had accidentally omitted. Most likely, ישב should be understood as a *hiphil* of שוב, paralleling מה ישב in the line below. ‖ 1QS [והואה והוא 4QS^j ‖ In 1QS, מצוררק is written as one word, and 4QS^j confirms the reading. Clines (1993–2014) lists the word under *[מצור] and emends and translates מצוררק (4QS^j) as "formation of spittle." For further discussion, see Alexander and Vermes 1998, 204. Qimron (2010, 230) reads מצירוק, but the letter preceding *qoph* in both 1QS and 4QS^j (see B-284305) is *resh*. ‖ **22** יבין is the last word in 1QS, but in 4QS^b the text continues with at least two lines, of which only little remains.

21 Born of a woman, what can he respond before you? He is kneaded from clay, and food of worms is his dwelling. He is a formation of spittle,
22 clay that is molded, and to dust is his longing. What can clay respond and the one molded by hand? What counsel can he understand?

---

22 In 4QS[b] this was not the last sentence of the Community Rule but the text seems to have continued there.

www.ingramcontent.com/pod-product-compliance
Lightning Source LLC
Chambersburg PA
CBHW082102230426
43670CB00017B/2926